ALTERNATIVE WORK SCHEDULES: INTEGRATING INDIVIDUAL AND ORGANIZATIONAL NEEDS

ALTERNATIVE WORK SCHEDULES: INTEGRATING INDIVIDUAL AND ORGANIZATIONAL NEEDS

ALLAN R. COHEN
HERMAN GADON
University of New Hampshire
The Whittemore School of Business and Economics

ADDISON-WESLEY PUBLISHING COMPANY
Reading, Massachusetts • Menlo Park, California
London • Amsterdam • Don Mills, Ontario • Sydney

This book is in the Addison-Wesley series:

ORGANIZATION DEVELOPMENT

Editors:
Edgar H. Schein
Richard Beckhard
Warren G. Bennis

ISBN 0-201-01052-6
ABCDEFGHIJK-DO-798

To Natasha and Joyce

FOREWORD

It has been five years since the Addison-Wesley series on organization development published the books by Roeber, Galbraith, and Steele, and it is almost ten years since the series itself was launched in an effort to define the then-emerging field of organization development. Almost from its inception the series enjoyed a great success and helped to define what was then only a budding field of inquiry. Much has happened in the last ten years. There are now dozens of textbooks and readers on OD; research results are beginning to accumulate on what kinds of OD approaches have what effects; educational programs on planned change and OD are growing; and there are regional, national, and even international associations of practitioners of planned change and OD. All of these trends suggest that this area of practice has taken hold and found an important niche for itself in the applied social sciences and that its intellectual underpinnings are increasingly solidifying.

One of the most important trends we have observed in the last five years is the connecting of the field of planned change and OD to the mainstream of organization theory, organizational psychology, and organizational sociology. Although the field has its roots primarily in these underlying disciplines, it is only in recent years that basic textbooks in "organization behavior" have begun routinely referring to organization development as an applied area that students and managers alike must be aware of.

The editors of this series have attempted to keep an open mind on the question of when the series has fulfilled its function and should be allowed to die. The series should be kept alive only as long as new areas of knowledge and practice central to organization development are emerging. During the last year or so, several such areas have been defined, leading to the decision to continue the series.

On the applied side, it is clear that information is a basic nutrient for any kind of valid change process. Hence, a book on data gathering, surveys, and feedback methods is very timely. Nadler has done an especially important service in this area in focusing on the variety of methods that can be used in gathering information and feeding it back to clients. The book is eclectic in its approach, reflecting the fact that there are many ways to gather information, many kinds to be gathered, and many approaches to the feedback process to reflect the particular goals of the change program.

Team building and the appropriate use of groups continues to be a second key ingredient of most change programs. So far no single book in the field has dealt explicitly enough with this important process. Dyer's approach will help the manager to diagnose when to use and not use groups and, most important, how to carry out team building when that kind of intervention is appropriate.

One of the most important new developments in the area of planned change is the conceptualizing of how to work with large systems to initiate and sustain change over time. The key to this success is "transition management," a stage or process frequently referred to in change theories, but never explored systematically from both a theoretical and practical point of view. Beckhard and Harris present a model that will help the manager to think about this crucial area. In addition, they provide a set of diagnostic and action tools that will enable the change manager in large systems to get a concrete handle on transition management.

The area of organization design has grown in importance as organizations have become more complex. Davis and Lawrence provide a concise and definitive analysis of that particularly elusive organization design—the matrix organization—and elucidate clearly its forms, functions, and modes of operation.

Problems of organization design and organization development are especially important in the rapidly growing form of organization known as the "multinational." Heenan and Perlmutter have worked in a variety of such organizations and review some fascinating cases as well as provide relevant theory for how to think about the design and development of such vastly more complex systems.

As organizations become more complex, managers need help in diagnosing what is going on both internally and externally. Most OD books put a heavy emphasis on diagnosing but few have provided workable schemes for managers to think through the multiple diagnostic issues that face them. Kotter has presented a simple and workable model that can lead the manager through a systematic diagnostic process while revealing the inherent complexity of organizations and the multiple interdependencies that exist within them.

Human resource planning and career development has become an increasingly important element in the total planning of organization improvement programs. Schein's book provides a broad overview of this field from the points of view of the individual and the total life cycle, the interaction between the career and other aspects of life such as the family, and the manager attempting to design a total human resource planning and development system.

The study of human resources in organizations has revealed the variety of new life styles and value patterns that employees of today display, forcing organizations to rethink carefully how they structure work and what they consider to be "normal" work patterns. Cohen and Gadon provide an excellent review of various alternative work patterns that have sprung up in the last decade and are revolutionizing the whole concept of a normal workweek.

It is exciting to see our field develop, expand, strengthen its roots, and grow outward in many new directions. I believe that the core theory or the integrative framework is not yet at hand, but that the varied activities of the theoreticians, researchers, and practitioners of planned change and OD are increasingly relevant not only to the change manager, but also to line managers at all levels. As the recognition grows that part of *every* manager's job is to plan, initiate, and manage change, so will the relevance of concepts and methods in this area come to be seen as integral to the management process itself. It continues to be the goal of this series to provide such relevant concepts and methods to managers. I hope we have succeeded in some measure in this new series of books.

March 1978   Edgar H. Schein

PREFACE

When we first became interested in alternative work schedules in 1971, they were generally viewed by many as simply additional benefits to make organizations more attractive to their employees. Although some literature on compressed workweeks and flexible working hours was beginning to appear, it was largely descriptive. Nor did we, like most others at the time, see in the schedules much more than a new and mildly interesting effort by personnel departments to try something different.

It soon became clear to us, however, that these schedules had in them a potential for producing widespread organizational change from the bottom up that was not understood and was therefore being overlooked. We believed we had discovered a tool for organizational development that had considerable significance.

Because we had started by looking at flexible working hours, which allowed the most day-to-day control for the individual, we were also slow to see that other schedule arrangements had similar potential. It was only when we began to ask *who* would benefit from particular schedule arrangements that we suddenly saw that a judicious offering of schedule choices could be both very freeing for individuals *and* helpful for organizations. We wanted this book to help others see the link between work schedules and the place of employees in the adult life cycle, so that more people could better the work/nonwork choices in their lives.

No book can be written without help from many others besides the authors. A number of people made valuable contributions to our thinking. Rosabeth Kanter and Barry Stein read an entire draft of the book and made many helpful suggestions regarding content and presentation. Linda Sprague helped ensure that we did not do great violence to the actual difficulties of those who do production scheduling, and lent personal expertise and materials on the compressed week. Alice Sargent, David Bradford, Bernhard Keppler, and John Veiga each read specific chapters and made useful suggestions. Betty Roberts helped us to see the relationship between middle age and career dropouts. And Allen Thompson served as a walking reference library, feeding us data and sources.

Several people from outside organizations generously offered specific examples from their own experiences or referred us to others. For this help we thank Diane Chartier and Kathy DeCambio of the Laconia, New Hampshire State School; Roger Hetherman, Kingsbury Machine Tool; Dave Johnson, Ashland Oil; Art Morrow, Davis and Furber; Sheila Mulcahy, University of Wisconsin; Barney Olmstead and Gretel Meier, New Ways to Work; Richard Sommerstadt, Control Data; Gayle Wells and Peter Janetos (with Marlene Goldberg and Diana Winn), John Hancock; Rita Williams, Alza Corporation; and Lynne Lipsitz, Social Security Administration.

We also want to give special thanks to Ed Schein for his original conceptual suggestions, which helped us see wider implications in our research, and for his support during our writing.

Two secretaries, and friends, who unfailingly managed to thread their way through our murky manuscripts and urgent rewrites, deserve extra thanks. The help of Jenifer McKinnon and Maddy Piper is integral to our work.

Finally, we want to acknowledge the intellectual and emotional support of Joyce Cohen and Natasha Josefowitz. During the writing of this manuscript each has gone from part-time to full-time work, providing us with personal incentive to understand the fit between work schedules and place in the life cycle. As fellow professionals with many interests in common with ours, they have been able to offer us invaluable comment.

Naturally, we take full responsibility for everything that is finally in the book, but we're grateful for all the help in getting there.

Durham, New Hampshire   A. R. C.
April 1978   H. G.

CONTENTS

1
CURRENT FORCES LEADING
TOWARD NEW SCHEDULES

Many people . . . desire an organization of work which acknowledges and facilitates what they must do (and want to do) in the
rest of their life. Work is no longer to be the inflexible core,
around which the other parts of life must bend. (Kanter, 1977b)

OVERVIEW

This book is written to help organizational leaders schedule work in a
way that better meets the needs of both the organization and individual employees. Individuals are increasingly pressuring organizations
to be more responsive to them as people with lives outside of work,
and have expressed great personal interest in alternative work schedules. At the same time, many organizations have found that offering
alternative scheduling arrangements has led to increases in morale,
commitment, availability of talented employees, and often productivity.

We will examine the forces affecting the choices of alternative
work schedules, the advantages and disadvantages of available
options, and individual needs as reflected through and predicted by
life-cycle stages. From this we develop a model for managers to use in
making choices about work patterns that will enhance the develop-

ment of the organization as well as its employees. Finally we look at the relationship between work schedule planning and organization development and offer guidelines to consultants for maximizing organization development payoffs from the introduction of new schedules.

INTRODUCTION

There is a growing body of literature on the issues surrounding individual career development and the stages of the adult life cycle (Schein, 1978). Though this material recognizes that individual personality contributes to the choices a person makes about work, career, commitment to one's employing organization, and willingness to work various hours, it shows that these choices tend to vary in predictable fashion over the course of an adult working life. At different life stages an individual will be preoccupied with different concerns, such as getting ahead in the organization, building warm, intimate family relationships, helping others grow and develop, testing self-capacities, or gracefully withdrawing from active participation in work life.

Concurrently, the last ten years have seen a proliferation of organizational efforts to vary the standard five-day, forty-hour workweek. Inventions such as the four-day workweek, staggered hours, flexible working hours, sabbaticals, permanent part-time work, and job sharing, which we call "alternative" work schedules, have spread rapidly. This spread is due at least partly to the many claims (increasingly substantiated by hard data) for organizational benefits, including increased productivity, increased morale, decreased absenteeism, lower turnover, and higher quality. In this book we will examine the links between these organizational innovations and the needs of individuals at different stages in their working lives, and show how organizations can take advantage of the knowledge accumulating in these two areas. We will use data from our own interviews and observations at banks, insurance, electronics, machine, drug, and retail companies, and county, federal, and state government agencies, as well as from a variety of published sources.

The first chapter discusses the environmental forces that create the interest in and pressure for new working arrangements. Chapter 2 shows how organizations can predict likely employee preferences for various schedules by using demographic data, especially information about the adult life and career cycles. Chapters 3, 4, and 5 examine the advantages and disadvantages of flexible and staggered working hours, the compressed week, and permanent part-time work (including job sharing). Chapter 6 develops a model for using the concepts in earlier chapters to select work schedules appropriate to both the needs of the organization and the preferences of employees. Finally, Chapter 7 shows how use of the alternative work arrangements and the scheduling methods we have developed may be implemented to maximize payoffs for further organization development efforts.

FORCES AFFECTING THE BEHAVIOR AND ATTITUDES OF INDIVIDUALS AND ORGANIZATIONS

A number of cultural, economic, and demographic forces have combined to lead a growing number of individuals to openly seek more flexibility in work schedules and more meaningful work. In turn, these forces and their effects on individuals have led organizations to look for ways to find new employees, to keep valued employees, and to increase individual and organizational productivity. The forces include changes in affluence, education, cultural attitudes, demographics, rate of participation in the labor force, employment rates, proportions of service workers, and the law. Let us look at them in detail.

Relative Affluence

While John Kenneth Galbraith's declaration that America is an affluent society appears to have been premature in light of the large number of people who either still remain below the poverty level or who are barely coping because of the world-wide recession and inflation of the last several years, the industrialized world is still relatively affluent. Many of life's privileges and comforts have become "necessities," accessible to vast numbers of those who work. Automobiles, which facilitate individual mobility and choice; television sets, which bring expensive entertainment and news into the home; telephones, which make interpersonal, as well as business, contact easy and instantly available; appliances, which reduce the the amount of time necessary for obtaining and preparing food and maintaining the house, are all commonplace. Many societies, now rich enough to afford health insurance, social security, and unemployment compensation, relieve some of the most severe forms of economic insecurity.

Education

United States society is becoming better educated at an astounding rate. Although the many definitions of adult education make measurement of its extent elusive, it is clear that it is pervasive and increasing.

The United States Office of Education (Wirtz, 1975) reports an increase in the number of "individuals in the civilian population, past compulsory school attendance age, who participate in part-time educational activities organized around some form of instruction," from 13 million in 1969 to 15.7 million in 1972. Many organizations already accommodate some of their employees' educational interests through tuition pay plans and educational leaves. In Germany, some companies have arranged to have courses offered on their own premises during the workday. Such arrangements have also been made for employees of the federal government in Washington, D.C.

The median number of school years completed by all persons over the age of twenty-five, 8.6 in 1940, has increased steadily since then: 9.3 in 1950, 10.5 in 1960, and 12.2 in 1970 (U.S. Department of Commerce, 1973). The number of college graduates in the labor force has increased from 10 percent in 1960 to 16.9 percent in 1975 and is expected to rise to 20–21 percent in 1985.

The diffusion of education throughout the society is enveloping both sexes, all ages, and minorities. In October 1976, 1.2 million persons over the age of thirty-five, including half again as many women as men, were enrolled in college, working toward a degree. Two-thirds of these "older" students were in the labor force, mostly seeking part-time work, though many were fully self-supporting. Many of the women were reeducating themselves in preparation for resuming their careers, or for undertaking one for the first time, after raising children (Young, 1977b).

Men, women, and minorities now enroll in college after high school in close to the same proportions, all approximately 50 percent (Young, 1977b). And with education come changes in attitudes and values.

Cultural Change

Greater affluence and education are part of broader cultural changes that affect the responses of those who work. It is clear that attitudes toward hierarchy and authority have changed fairly dramatically in the last twenty-five years. Surveys by Yankelovitch (1974a) show that there has been a growing preference for alternative life-styles, more self-control, and more interesting work.

Change has been promoted by the pervasiveness and immediacy of mass media, improved transportation, and readily accessible lines of communication. The last ten to fifteen years have been marked by a growing consciousness of the possibilities of individual fulfillment—in life in general and at work. The proliferation of therapy, consciousness raising, and religious movements has reinforced the idea that self-fulfillment is possible and desirable—and perhaps deserved. Large proportions of college students studied by Yankelovich (1974b) believed that they were *entitled*, as a social right, to participate in decisions that affect one's own work (56 percent), the right to work (27 percent), and a minimum income (26 percent); 17 percent even thought they were entitled to an interesting job.

As the work force becomes more homogeneous in terms of educational background, it will become more difficult for employers to justify selection on the basis of educational differentials. Better educated employees will, in all likelihood, see themselves as also entitled to the interesting work that has historically been available to those relative few whose educational advantage had entitled them to it. For the first time since the 1920s, there has been a reversal of the migration from rural to urban areas. Most of the migrants from cities appear to be in search of a more satisfying life-style and more personally challenging, autonomous work (Gallese, 1977).

The inclination of industrialized countries to minimize unemployment and its effects as a matter of social policy reinforces expectations that work should be meaningful. The "right to work" is increasingly expressed as a national goal. Welfare payments and unemployment benefits have risen dramatically and provide an undergirding of support for those without sources of income. Such "transfer payments" in the United States, including social security, have risen from $45 billion in 1965, to $192 billion in 1975, an increase of 430 percent, amounting to about one-fifth of total wages and salaries!

The promise of some minimum level of economic security, which allows a person to be more selective, combined with higher aspirations growing out of more education, has changed attitudes toward work. Those who can get along for periods of time without work are more likely to be choosy than those for whom earning a living is a necessity. Employers are being forced to find new methods of attracting and managing those who are less dependent or insecure, more concerned about satisfaction at work, and more determined to exert control over their lives.

An Aging Population

Another force affecting attitudes and creating readiness for alternative work schedules is that of basic demographic trends. The population of the United States is aging as the birthrate declines steadily from the high watermark of twenty-six per 1,000 in 1955 to the present level of fourteen per 1,000. Projections for the future do not anticipate a reversal of the trend, though there is an indication of a slight rise in births by women in their thirties who had postponed families.

The number of people over sixty-five is also rising. In 1975, one out of ten persons in the total population was over sixty-five, compared to one out of twenty-five in 1900. In 1955, there was one retired person receiving old age benefits for every seven persons working. In 1960, it was one out of four, and in 1974, one out of three. In the year 2000 it is likely to be one out of two, unless present circumstances affecting retirement decisions change.

Labor Force Participation

Despite the aging population in general, however, the current work force has had an influx of new, younger participants. These trends in labor force participation rates suggest the likelihood that pressure for access to more opportunity for meaningful work will be reinforced. (The labor force participation rate is calculated by dividing the number of persons in a particular category who are looking for work by the number of persons in that category in the total population.) Three rates stand out most dramatically.

First, women have increased their rate of participation from one-third in 1950 to almost half (47.4 percent) in 1976. And almost half of all married women are now working. In 1950, women accounted for 29.6 percent of the total civilian labor force as compared to 39.6 percent in 1976 (Employment and Training Report of the President, 1976).

Second, teenagers have sought work in greater numbers, up from 5.2 million in 1960 to 9.2 million in 1974.

Third, there is a decreasing work-force participation rate of persons aged fifty-five to sixty-four. They have been dropping out of the work force in greater numbers, from 13.1 percent in 1950, to 17 percent in 1970, and to 24.2 percent in 1976 (Etzioni, 1977).

Thus, even while the general population is aging, there has been an influx of women and teenagers into the work force, and a reduction in the numbers of older workers. This has resulted in considerable change in the composition of the work force, furthering the changes in attitudes toward work described earlier.

Employment Rate

A number of conflicting forces are being felt in the marketplace. The rising rate of participation in the labor force by women and the young presents the haunting specter of continued high levels of unemployment, borne especially by the present disadvantaged. Furthermore, the increasing dropout rate of people aged fifty-five to sixty-four may be offset by the desire of about one-third of current retirees over sixty-five to work if allowed (*Newsweek*, 1977). The pending legislation in Congress to prohibit compulsory retirement at age sixty-five reflects the aversion of many older people to total withdrawal from the labor force as well as concern by those who work about financially supporting the growing proportion of over-sixty-fives.

In addition, those who are retiring early often do not wish to completely remove themselves from the work force. Either they cannot (for health reasons) or do not wish to work full time but would gladly work if convenient part-time schedules could be arranged, or they do not choose to continue at work that is meaningless, degrading, or out of their control yet would like to have jobs where they choose the nature of the work and its hours. Also, even though the dropping birthrate after 1955 will compensate somewhat for the high rate of participation of teenagers in the labor force, it seems clear that there are dangers in failing to provide young people with more employment opportunities than they have had in the past. Increasing concern with the urban crime rate, which is associated with teenage unemployment, and the plight of blacks in the inner city, suggest that the 10–20-percent unemployment rate for white teenagers and the 20–40-percent rate for black teenagers sustained through much of the 1970s will not continue to be tolerable.

Adding to the problems for those who are least employable is the increased education rate mentioned earlier. While almost half of all high school graduates in 1976 went to college (compared to one out of ten in 1940), there has not been a corresponding increase in jobs requiring a college background (Young, 1977a). By 1985, the shortfall in jobs that traditionally require a college degree is variously estimated at from 1.6 million to 6–8 million (Best and Stern, 1977). Since a 1971 survey conducted for the U.S. Department of Labor (Quinn and Sheppard) indicated that one-fourth to one-third of persons in the work force already identified themselves as overeducated for their jobs, the potential for dissatisfaction and resulting pressure for opportunities for fuller utilization of one's abilities is considerable.

There is, therefore, pressure from some groups to reduce the number competing for work, and pressure from others to provide them with opportunities they have not yet had.

Even if jobs can be provided, and this will be no mean accomplishment, a better educated, more secure work force is likely to find them relatively unacceptable unless access to the more rewarding ones is made easier than in the past. Given the present intolerance of inequality, reflected in organized efforts by pressure groups to produce change, continuation of the ways in which employment has grown in the last fifteen or so years is not likely to be acceptable. Table 1.1 illustrates the problem. It shows that the growth in employment since 1960 has largely been in low-earnings jobs, relegated essentially to women and the young.

Table 1.1

Percentage Distribution of the Labor Force by Earning Classification, 1960 and 1970

	Job Category by Earnings Distribution					
Characteristic	1960			1970		
	High	Medium	Low	High	Medium	Low
Total labor force	22.0	42.0	36.0	21.0	33.0	46.0
Age and sex						
Mature men	32.0	43.8	24.1	32.8	41.0	26.2
Young men	12.0	42.0	46.0	12.9	32.0	55.1
Mature women	8.4	36.9	57.4	7.7	23.4	69.4
Young women	3.3	38.2	58.4	4.7	19.0	77.0

Source: Marcia Freedman, *Labor Markets: Segments and Shelters* (New York: Allanheld, Osmun, 1976), p. 75.

There is likely to be increasing difficulty in getting people to accept low-level jobs. Younger people will not readily accept authoritarian behavior and want meaning from and control of work. Coupled with the decline in numbers of teenagers available to enter the work force in the 1980s, there is likely to be great difficulty in filling low-level, traditionally organized and scheduled jobs (Sheppard, 1976).

Yet even while some members of the work force are looking for opportunities to extend work, others want to trade income for time off. In a survey conducted by the Roper Organization in 1974, blue-collar workers, white-collar workers, union members, the affluent, and professionals indicated a preference for long leaves, sabbaticals, and shorter hours over other benefits (*Roper Reports,* 1974). In still another survey of 791 employees of Alameda County, California in 1976, 80 percent of them chose a career cycle that gave them extended periods of schooling and free time throughout their working lives in preference to their present career cycle of school-work-retirement. In Santa Clara County, California, employees can choose among these different plans: (1) retention of existing hours and pay; (2) a 5-percent reduction in income in exchange for 10½ days off; (3) a 10-percent reduction in income for 21 days off; or (4) a 20-percent reduction in income for two periods of 21 days off. In the first nine months of the plan, about 17 percent of the county's work force took off between 5 percent and 10 percent of their previous work time. Thus the younger, older, and female segments of the work force, which have been growing, "often prefer shorter hours to additional income" (Levitan and Belous, 1977).

It may well be that those who want to work less can be accommodated to the benefit of those who desire greater opportunity. New scheduling options, allowing for better fit between employee desires and timing of work, can help deal with the conflicting pressures over employment opportunities.

In speculating about the effects of widespread provision of new scheduling options, Best and Stern (1977) calculate a reduction in unemployment of 1 percent, if half of the labor force were to exchange 2 percent of their income for one additional paid week of vacation, or if 7 percent of the work force exchanged one-seventh of their wages for one paid year off every seven years. The Roper survey and the survey of workers in Alameda County cited above, and the recent willingness of union members to exchange wages for more time off, as noted below, indicate that new scheduling options could be attractive to the public at large. If they were widely adopted, they could reduce unemployment significantly, *and* address the need for more equal distribution of more desirable work.

In efforts to cope with the need to share opportunity, the United Auto Workers (UAW) and Communications Workers of America (CWA) have negotiated a substantial number of extra days off each year. In 1977, the second year of their contract with General Motors, UAW members will average 35.5 days off with pay.

What we are witnessing, of course, is a trade-off of nonwork time for increased pay. Whether or not this presages a new shift downward in average weekly hours of work is perhaps too soon to tell. Nevertheless, these union-management agreements represent a consciousness of a need to share opportunity, even at the cost of some material well-being for many persons directly affected.

The trade-off of income for time off is, however, in the historical tradition of developing industrial economies. The average workweek in the United States dropped from 58.9 hours in 1901 to roughly 40 hours in 1948, where it has remained virtually unchanged to the present.

At the same time, the average number of hours worked by married *couples* has been increasing since the 1940s, as increasing numbers of married women joined the work force. And with overtime and moonlighting, there are large segments of the labor force for whom more hours are spent working and commuting than the average workweek hours would suggest.

In the case of those working extra hours, there is a natural need for flexible schedules in order to accommodate to life needs; for others, there is likely to be a continued desire for reduced hours, or at least more usable leisure hours.

The breaking of the lock-step education-work-retirement cycle is already generating new opportunities for employment as well as non-work activities, and much more pressure in that direction is likely.

Shift to Service Work

While all of these employment trends and cross-trends were unfolding, America became a service economy, changing the nature of jobs available. Work continues to shift away from manufacturing toward professional, clerical, and service occupations. Figure 1.1 shows the

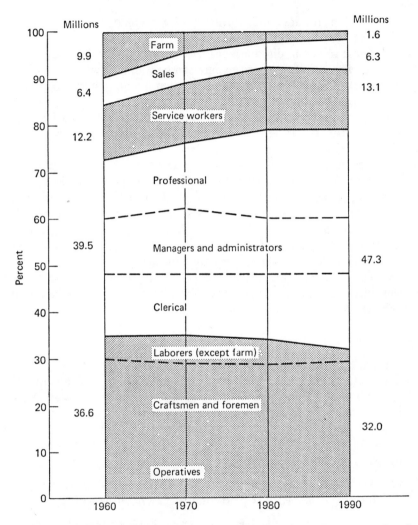

Fig. 1.1 Change in distribution of employment by major occupational group. (*Source: Manpower Report of the President,* 1975.)

extent to which nonmanufacturing work has come to predominate in America.

These trends in distribution of work increase the likelihood that alternative scheduling arrangements can be widely adopted, since service work is often less interdependent than manufacturing work and thus allows individual flexibility. The more independently work is performed, the easier it is to offer the choice of a variety of work schedules. Even work in the manufacturing sector includes much clerical and service work with relatively low levels of interdependence.

No work in an organization, of course, stands wholly by itself. The contrast is between the kind of work done by file clerks, for example, who can acquire, store, and place file material by themselves without particularly affecting others so long as reasonable time limits are met for completion of the work, and the work done by people on a linear assembly line (as, for instance, automobiles) that does not have buffer stocks and has a short cycle time for each operation.

Thus, the trend away from manufacturing work can facilitate the sharing of employment opportunities and promote the equalization of access to more rewarding work.

The Law

All that has been said about pressures for change toward more equal opportunity, choice, and self-control is reflected in the sanction of law. It is clear that in the United States in the seventies, the work place has become a main arena for the stimulation of social change. Five federal measures in particular serve unfailing notice on employers that the needs of a large part of society, needs that were not attended to in the past, must now be served. These are as follows:

1. The Equal Pay Act of 1963, which requires that employees performing equal work be paid equal wages, regardless of sex

2. Title VII of the Civil Rights Act of 1964, as amended, which makes illegal any discrimination in wages, terms, conditions, and privileges of employment by employers, employment agencies, labor unions, and joint labor-management committees, because of race, color, religion, sex, or national origin

3. Executive Order 11246 of 1965, which prohibits discrimination in employment on the basis of race, color, religion, or national origin by contractors on federal or federally assisted projects

4. Public Law 90-202, the Age Discrimination in Employment Act, which prohibits discrimination on the basis of age between the ages of forty and sixty-five

5. Title IX of the Education Amendments of 1972, which prohibits sex discrimination against students and employees in most educational programs or activities receiving federal financial aid.

These laws legitimate the claims of a large number of persons to a better life and provide them with pathways to it. Increasing recourse to the courts reflects awareness of the potential of these newly available means to achieve change. The reliance on litigation is reinforced by other provisions and the extensive use of them, such as by environmental groups taking advantage of the Executive Order that created the Environmental Protection Agency (EPA), and safety-minded persons who seek enforcement of the provisions of the Occupational Safety and Health Act (OSHA). The litigious society is upon us.

IMPLICATIONS

Thus a number of forces lead to increased pressure on organizations to respond to individual needs and cause many employees to be more selective in terms of when, for how long, for whom, and how hard they are willing to work. The law, increasing affluence, the spread of education, an aging work force, a greater percentage of women and young people seeking work, are all generating pressure to provide more choice and equalization of opportunity. Changing cultural norms, which tolerate a greater range of life-styles, a willingness of persons at different times in their lives to exchange time off for extra pay, and the continued shift away from the heavily interdependent jobs in manufacturing suggest that the move to alternative work schedules is becoming both easier and more appealing.

As a recurring theme, the need persists for means of making more jobs available by redistributing opportunity. In order to relieve the pressure to redistribute opportunity, there will inevitably be recourse to alternative schedules, as well as continued experimentation with other employment constructs such as job enrichment and autonomous work groups. Alternative work schedules will not only allow individuals to integrate family, recreational, and educational needs with their work lives, but may also spread work over more persons.

All of the methods for rearranging work time are ways of dealing with the trade-offs individuals make between work and nonwork activities. Human beings have always had to make such trade-offs—even if only to sleep fitfully in caves before resuming the hunt—though the cave paintings at Lascaux, France and elsewhere suggest that people always did more than just work, sleep, and procreate.

In the days before there were "organizations" more complex than the family, work and other activities were probably determined largely by the natural rhythms of the weather. Activities varied by season, but also within the day. In very hot countries work often started early, as it still does, was suspended during the hottest midday hours, then resumed in the late afternoon until dark. This is somewhat different from the daily pattern in more temperate climates.

Modern organizational life since the industrial revolution tends to be less dependent on the weather and daylight hours, though work patterns, tempo, and vacations are often still based on agrarian habits and timing, even when not technologically necessary. Since 1900, work schedules have become standardized for most of the labor force. Among wage and salary workers, about 70 percent are on standard schedules of thirty-five to forty-two hours a week (Owen, 1976).

In recent years, the trade-off questions have become more conscious, by individuals as well as organizations. Organizations have been asking whether different patterns of work times will lead to greater productivity, ease of operations, or acquisition of talent. Individuals, well past the sheer need for constant work in order to survive, have been asking whether a rearrangement of their own work timing patterns would be more fulfilling. As a result, during the past ten years, a proliferation of new patterns has been developed (or rediscovered), tried, modified, and disseminated.

No matter how complex the variations, and they can be quite complex as we shall see, they can be described as varying along three dimensions:

1. The degree to which nonwork time is taken daily or aggregated in longer periods

2. The degree to which work is less than what is currently considered "full" time (forty to forty-four hours per week)

3. The degree to which the individual controls the timing of the trade-offs.

Pressures in our society are altering employee demands and expectations and pushing organizations to invent or adopt work schedules and other arrangements that fit better with employee preferences. The pressures confront us with important individual and organizational issues. From the individual point of view, the central question is: *How can I find interesting, satisfying work that will allow me to balance my personal life with the demands of the job?* From the organization's perspective, the central question is: *What can we do to attract committed, effective employees to do what needs to be done at the appropriate times?* This book addresses these questions and their interconnection.

2
A MODEL LINKING CAREER AND LIFE-CYCLE STAGES TO ATTITUDES ABOUT WORK

CASSIE

Oh, Zach, I didn't mind not being part of your work. I loved you, I could have handled that. It was not being a part of your life that got to me. And not being able to keep up with you. Because that's what you expected. I know you did. You were moving up and you wanted me to move right up there with you. Well, I was a good dancer, but you wanted me to be a star.

ZACH

What's wrong with that? Why shouldn't you be? Why shouldn't you be the best you can be? When I got out of the chorus I decided I was going to . . .

CASSIE

Zach, that's not a decision, that's a disease. God, good, better, best!—I hate it. How can you stand it? You live by it—and you're stuck with it. Are you gonna go from one show to the next to the next rehearsing them all for twenty-four hours a day for the rest of your life? (Bennett, Dante, and Kirkwood, 1975)

ATTITUDES TOWARD WORK AND LEISURE

Not everyone feels the same about work. Some people literally cannot get enough of it, and seem to live to work. Such "workaholics" are often the butt of jokes, but many companies value the person who puts work ahead of family—as long as family cooperates (Kanter, 1977a).

Others, in increasing numbers, as noted in Chapter 1, work only to live and will choose to avoid work whenever they can survive without it. There are many who, like some Hippies of the 1960s, put leisure ahead of work—and invest considerable time and energy in making leisure enjoyable.

In between these two extremes, every variation may be found. There are those who work hard and play hard. Some will only invest in "meaningful" or challenging work; others will work hard at any assignment because it is the "right thing to do." Many place family needs above work even when work is satisfying.

It is probably possible to explain attitudes toward work and leisure on an individual, intrapsychic basis, using psychoanalytic investigation into early childhood experiences, tests of self-concept, and the like. But apart from the scientific validity of such methods, they are slow, expensive, and not easily accessible. Organizations need easier, more convenient ways of assessing the likely attitudes toward work of their existing and potential work forces. Such information is useful not only for making location or relocation decisions, but also for sizing up opportunities inherent in the interests of available employees, estimating the likely success of attracting good employees to shift work, and determining work schedules that meet the needs of employees.

As we shall demonstrate, there are many possible variations from the standard 9 to 5, forty-hour week work schedules, variations that can allow people to better adjust their working and leisure activities to their preferences. It is the basic hypothesis of this book that the more closely people's work schedules match the timing and amount of their desires for work and leisure, the greater will be their commitment to, and performance at, work.*

---

* Empirical research has not yet definitely established a direct and inevitable link between commitment and performance because of intervening variables such as the organization's stress on achievement, employee's ability, the clarity of the employee's organizational role, and the activeness of the commitment (Steers, 1977). Also, some routine jobs may be equally well-performed by uncommitted employees (Davis and Walton, 1977). Thus in its purest form the hypothesis should take all of these factors into account. Nevertheless, it is unlikely that greater commitment would lead to lesser performance, so we can comfortably hold such refinements aside. Regardless of work schedules, organizational concern for achievement, or role clarity, employee ability and active commitment are desirable in and of themselves.

In matching persons with work a number of relevant factors have been excluded in recent years from consideration as a basis of employee selection and promotion. They include age and sex by law, and family status by custom. The obvious purpose of these changing legal and informal norms is to extend opportunities to substantial numbers in our society to whom they had previously been denied.

Paradoxically, the mind set produced by such social objectives may screen out of people's thinking some organizational innovations that are most likely to fit the needs of individuals as a function of age, sex, and family status. Thus the effort to extend opportunities in some areas may also turn out to limit them in others.

Since there are advantages to knowing the likely preferences of available and potential employees for timing and amounts of work, it would be useful to develop methods for economically and rapidly estimating such preferences. We believe that recent work on the adult life cycle and on career stages, coupled with selected demographic data, can provide useful working tools for assessing attitudes about work.

ADULT DEVELOPMENT AND CAREER PATHS

Patterns of behavior associated with stages of adult aging have been suggested by numerous studies (Erickson, 1959; Levinson, 1977; Gould, 1975; Roberts, 1975), and have been summarized by Schein (1978). These are descriptive rather than normative and deeply embedded in the socioeconomic context of our culture. Should the environment change, the patterns would likely change. For example, a shift in values that encourages women to pursue careers in the same manner as men, accompanied by more equal opportunities to do so, would probably be followed by a shift away from the pattern of behavior associated with the present tendency for late entry (age thirty-five to forty-five) of many women into the work force. Should the cycle of education-work-forced retirement be altered, the behavior currently associated with career paths would change. So the age-related cycles are only descriptions of likely tendencies under current conditions, not inevitabilities. But they are a convenient starting place for our analysis.

THEORY OF LIFE CYCLES

Studies of persons at different stages of their adult lives suggest that there are behavioral patterns into which people generally fall. These are marked by periods of transition following periods of stability of approximately seven years. In the popular notion of the "seven-year itch," the folk wisdom has anticipated the scholarly conclusions of the social scientist. It is discoveries like this that once prompted George Homans to write that the task of the social scientist is to document common sense and identify the conditions that make it a reliable guide to action (Homans, 1961).

The age differentiated periods that seem to represent these alternating periods of stability and transition for men are outlined in Table 2.1.

The stages of development shown in Table 2.1 were induced from studies of *men* at work, including professionals, managers, and blue- and white-collar workers. Women seem to follow different and more complex patterns of development that are related to their childbearing functions (Sheehy, 1974). If they enter the work force in their twenties and remain without children they seem to follow a course similar to that of men. They experiment, test themselves, and begin to establish their place in the outside world of work. In the early thirties, they too pause, as do men, to review their accomplishments and decide where to direct their next burst of energy. Whereas men often dig in hard for a major push for achievement at work, the working woman tends to pause to think about having children before it is too late. While some continue to work full time whether or not they have children (or marry), many drop out to attend to family, home, and husband. If still available for work after having children, it is on a more limited basis. Approximately ten years later they will again be thinking of a full-time commitment to work and career.

Though an increasing number of women delay both marriage and children, the large number of them still follow traditional patterns of behavior. They marry in their twenties and have children. If they stay in the work force, they tend to prefer flexibility and/or part-time work. Their family is their high priority. If felt, the need for self-development is postponed. More often it is undiscovered, awaiting emergence in the thirties, after the last child has left for school. It is then that women become available for work, often for the first time, ready to devote themselves to the exploration of an occupational identity.

The situation for women is further complicated by the increasing rate of divorce, which leaves many of them with small children needing care. Because divorced women with children often do not have

Table 2.1
Stages of Adult Development (Males)

Age	Stage	Description of Behavior and Attitudes
16/17–22/23	Breaking out—experimentation with adulthood	Testing behavior, reaching out and withdrawing, challenging authority. Need to leave home and enter the adult world.
22–28	Establishing self in the adult world	Exploring work, abilities, interests, relationships.
28–33	Age 30—time of transition	Review of accomplishments. Reconsideration of commitments to work and to relationships. High rate of divorce and occupational change.
30/33–39/40	Settling down as a member of society, as a family member, as a career aspirant or job holder	Life potential clearer, efforts redirected toward career push if upwardly mobile or friends and family if "stuck" on job.
36+	Alone as an adult	Awareness of larger responsibilities for family including increasing need to provide care for own parents, rather than vice versa, thus beginning of role reversals. Self-sufficiency at work and responsibility for newcomers—sponsorship, nurturance.
40–45	Midlife transition	"Life begins at 40." Acceptance of own limits. Reassessment of potential. Reevalu-

Age	Stage	Description of Behavior and Attitudes
		ation of priorities, of work and leisure, of family and work, of the soft and the hard sides of self.
		Consideration of alternatives: drop out, reeducation, acceptance, resignation, shifting emphasis, affirmation of life as is.
43–50	Restabilization	Renewed interest in relationships, travel, hobbies, leisure. Increased acceptance of self, work, life's circumstances. Relative freedom from care of children. Awareness of and interest in young persons at work and play.
50–55	Nurturance of others	Concern for others—children, grandchildren.
55–65	Anticipation of retirement	Planning disengagement, consideration of early retirement, phasing out. Search for fitting work, appropriate work schedules, companions, communities. Redefining relationships at work, with children, with friends.
65+	Postretirement	Drop out of work force. Search for substitutes for work: leisure, hobbies, relationships, meaningful task activities—social, economic, work.

enough money to provide for their family, they frequently need permanent full-time jobs, but preferably with a lot of flexibility.

The statistics on the actual rate and kind of participation in the work force by women do not necessarily reflect their preferences. If good child care, for instance, was more accessible, more women might work and also feel freer to pursue careers differently. There is some indication in the Swedish experience, which includes paternity leave and a higher tolerance for role reversals, that the life cycles of women would more closely approximate those of men if they had more alternatives from which to choose.

Though we rely on an analysis of the present legal, cultural, and normative characteristics of our society to predict the preferences of women as well as men for work schedules, we do not thereby suggest that we think that the sex-role norms of our society are equitable. On the contrary, it has consistently been our position that increasing the range of choice for *all* persons is desirable. Not only does it enrich their lives but it tends as well to increase their commitment to work.

CAREERS—A DEVELOPMENTAL CONCEPT

The study of adult life cycles suggests that people have particular behavioral tendencies at different times in their lives. The study of careers is concerned with the behavioral tendencies of people at work, affected in part by their development as adults. Careers too can be traced through developmental sequences (Schein, 1971, 1978; Van Maanen and Schein, 1977; Super, 1957):

1. Exploration Stage

   This is a period of preparation for work, affected by opportunities present and perceived, characterized by testing and tentativeness.

2. Establishment Stage (Early Career)

   a) *Mutual recruitment.* This is a period of getting started, searching for a job, being tested, and facing acceptance and rejection.

   b) *Acceptance and entry.* This is a time of socialization, beginning formation of an occupational identity, and fear of failure.

c) *First job assignment.* This is a time of discovery of the world of work, of the pleasure of achievement, of the realization of constraints, of tentative commitments to occupation and organization, and of efforts to prove oneself.

d) *Leveling off, transfer, and/or promotion.* This is a time of settling on a direction, of realizing the presence or absence of a potential, of feeling stuck or on the move, and of discovering the tedium and boredom of repetition.

e) *Granting of tenure.* This is a time of evaluation by the organization leading to a commitment to an individual, release, or side-tracking. If accepted, self-esteem is enhanced. If rejected, self-reassessment leads to resignation and withdrawal, or change and efforts to find new directions.

3. Maintenance Stage

a) *Mid-career.* This is the time for occurrence of the midlife crisis that follows from self-reexamination in the presence of security. With potential for new growth or relaxation, imagination is necessary to stimulate renewed contributions and commitment to organizational effectiveness.

4. Late Career

This is a time for teaching rather than striving, of deceleration at work, of growing interests in nonwork activities, of the rediscovery of off-the-job relationships.

5. Decline

This is a time of preparation for retirement, of decreasing responsibility, of increasing reliance on wisdom gleaned from experience, and of acceptance of one's self.

To the extent that careers are oriented toward upward mobility, progress and stage of development are related to age. Attaining a position or title that is seen as appropriate for a given age is in fact often necessary in order to keep upwardly mobile. Therefore, the late starter, or the person with an interrupted career, may find that opportunities are scarce. Women, in particular, face this problem since many of them only begin "exploring" in their thirties, or attempting "reentry" in their forties (Kanter 1977a).

Although studies of careers cover persons in all kinds of occupations, the characteristics of hourly jobs tend to be far more constraining than ones in the professions, the arts, and management.

The differences emerge quite clearly from a review of a study by Schein (1975, 1978) that suggests that persons develop themes, over a lifetime, that govern their choices of occupation and institution. These themes are called "career anchors." A career anchor is defined as a "syndrome of self-perceived talents, values, and motives that organize and give stability to career-oriented decisions and that probably provide one key element of an individual's sense of identity." Examining the careers of forty-four graduates of the Sloan School of Management at the Massachusetts Institute of Technology, Schein selected the following anchors as representing the alternative orienting foci of their careers:

1. Managerial competence—representing the exercise of leadership, authority, and power without internal conflict; e.g., chief executive officer.

2. Technical/functional competence—representing the use of special knowledge, expertise, talent; e.g., engineers, controllers, scientists.

3. Security—representing the need for stability, continuity, income maintenance; e.g., civil service work, work in a more stable organization.

4. Creativity—representing the need to invent, create, build, be original, new; e.g., entrepreneurs, artists, some professions such as architecture.

5. Autonomy and independence—representing the need to be free from controls and to be self-directing; e.g., professors, consultants.

These themes are not seen as definitive by Schein, nor by any means appropriate for all occupations. For lower prestige jobs some of the themes might not apply and new ones would have to be developed.

Security is a concept that does seem to apply as well to large numbers of hourly workers. For many hourly workers, the "job" loses its identity and becomes mainly a means of providing for the family. This is reflected in the inability of some children of blue-collar families to identify their parents with their work. The parents' identities are defined instead by other terms, largely around their roles in the family. One such characterization heard from a twenty-year-old in a strongly ethnic household was reference to his father as Mr. Outside, and to his mother as Mrs. Inside. "Outside" and "inside" were this young man's primary identification of his parents.

Autonomy and independence certainly represent a preference of many hourly workers, a fact reflected in survey results that consistently show that workers strongly prefer freedom from close supervision.

Stability is a probable "anchor" for many hourly workers. This notion emerges from the reflections by George Strauss (1974) about the reasons that blue-collar workers for years have indicated quite high satisfaction with their jobs while clearly being dissatisfied with their *work* (*Work in America*, 1973). We suggest that a need for adjustment requires acceptance of tedious, boring work and the expectation that satisfactions must be found off the job. Thus, attitude toward work becomes apathetic, but its stability provides relief from anxiety.

Strauss's conclusions are consistent with findings of differentiated reactions to the task features of job enrichment—autonomy, skill variety, task identity, and task significance (Hackman and Oldham, 1975). Contrary to the popular notion that workers *generally* will respond with more satisfaction, motivation, and commitment to enriching changes in task features of their jobs, Van Maanen and Katz (1974) found that it was not so for those who had been assigned the same job for at least fifteen years. It was only young persons just starting out who felt that increased task significance was meaningful and did make their work more satisfying. For hourly workers who have been on a job for fifteen or twenty years, the frustration of the work place is apparently accepted as the price, the sacrifice, to be made in affirmation of the role as the family provider. The relatively minor expansion of essentially dull work that holds little promise of continuing challenge provides little lasting satisfaction (Strauss, 1974).

Furthermore, Rosabeth Kanter (1977a) has argued that it is *opportunity* per se that is motivating even more than the task itself.

Thus for those who perceive no increased opportunity for advancement from job enrichment, stability may be a more certain and satisfying basis for action.

Yankelovich (1974a) attributes the favorable response to increases in task significance of young blue-collar, entry-level employees to a shift of values toward a "yearning to find self-fulfillment through meaningful work." The difference that age makes, he says, is between the "wish" and the "demand" for fulfillment. Young people, it seems, are less cynical than older ones. For them meaningfulness at work is a realistic expectation (entitlement) and can therefore be demanded. Older people, believing that work will not be meaningful because it cannot or will not be provided by their employers, wish for it but do not expect it.

In summary, when assessing likely employee responses to work innovations, especially scheduling alternatives, it is valuable to consider employees' place in the career cycle and their prevailing career anchors as well as their place in the life cycle. In addition, integration of the knowledge of adult life cycles and career cycles with certain other demographic factors should help organizations predict the interest of present or potential employees in different work schedules, and therefore aid them in planning to use manpower more effectively. Additional information of importance in predicting attitudes includes the nature of the work, employment of spouse, socioeconomic status, race, sex, education, health, and geography.

NATURE OF THE EMPLOYEE'S WORK

The nature of one's work will influence attitudes toward it, satisfaction with it, commitment to it, and motivation for it. For managerial and professional personnel who have worked since they left school and are doing well, the thirties may be a time of consolidation and concentration of effort for a big push to get to the top. These persons are committed to work, often to the neglect of family and leisure. They are satisfied with it, highly motivated, and willing to work long hours at a time in order to get ahead. Managers who are dead-ended, and cannot look forward to upward mobility, have coping mechanisms, which include not only turning to families but also hoarding power or building interpersonal gossip networks (Kanter, 1977a).

For those individuals who are looking outside of work for satisfaction, whether they are managers who are stuck or hourly workers resigned to boring work, *flexibility*, in order to accommodate themselves to family and outside interests, and/or large blocks of leisure time, becomes increasingly attractive. The union drive for more days off and shorter work weeks with full pay, as represented by UAW contracts with the automobile companies (which now provide twenty-seven nonwork days during the year, of which twelve are "personal days" taken at the discretion of the employee but planned with the company), reflects the wish of individuals for larger blocks of leisure time as well as the union's interest in spreading the work.

EMPLOYMENT OF SPOUSE AND FAMILY SITUATION

A problem faced by couples after their mid-thirties, if the wife makes a late entry into the work force, is the reconciliation of the different phases of the cycle they are in. Often when the man is turning toward family and a reordering of priorities, the wife is making commitments to work, and discovering new relationships.

Reconciliation is often particularly difficult when work schedules prevent couples from integrating their various needs in ways that would be most suitable for them. Thus whether or not employees have working spouses affects desires for scheduling alternatives. Choices of times of arrivals and departures at work (flexible working hours), part-time work, job sharing, and sabbaticals would give couples options that could minimize the strain on their relationship.

The presence or absence of children and of a spouse also plays a major role in affecting attitudes toward work schedules. Single parents have greater need for variation in schedule then do parents with spouses.

SOCIOECONOMIC STATUS

Persons with few skills or skills of a lower order, those on welfare, and/or those from disadvantaged minorities find fewer opportunities for employment. Often, necessity makes them available for part-time work at odd hours, though many would happily work full time if they could find jobs at all, or at least jobs with any promise of advancement. For many, low-paying, dead-end jobs are worse than no jobs at all, since welfare, food stamps, and/or unemployment compensation are no more degrading and leave more unencumbered time.

MINORITY STATUS

Laws such as have been passed by the state of Massachusetts mandating permanent part-time work and flextime for a given percentage of state jobs recognize the need for these schedules to provide work for deprived minorities. Alternatives to the fixed, standard schedule have an obvious appeal to single heads of households, who more often than not are women and/or black. Though permanent part-time work and flexible hours are by no means comprehensive answers to the problem of inequality, they do present deprived persons with new and previously unavailable opportunities to live and work.

SEX

A number of examples of sex combined with other circumstances have already been presented to suggest the likely appeal to individuals of different work schedules. For women, in particular, three factors deserve repeating. First, women are often late entrants into the work force. Second, a significant proportion start, drop out, and later seek reentry. Third, married women in increasing numbers, presently forty-four out of one hundred, seek work. Their preferences for work schedules depend substantially on a number of characteristics of their lives. For example, young mothers with children in school seem to prefer flexible working hours and/or part-time work so that they can see their children off to school and be home when they return. Clearly, compressed workweeks would not be preferred by them under these circumstances.

EDUCATION

The traditional sequence of education-work-retirement shows signs of changing. Education is becoming a lifelong experience. The wish for it, or need for it as skills obsolesce or careers become atrophied, stimulates interest in sabbaticals and extended vacations, flexible working hours, and part-time work, and, in some cases (as when MBA degrees can be pursued in weekend programs, such as at Rutgers or the University of Chicago), in compressed work weeks.

Furthermore, teenagers in school are increasingly interested in part-time work. In 1960, 34 percent were in the work force. In 1970 this percentage had risen to 40 percent, and employment of boys and girls sixteen to nineteen years of age had risen 2½ times as fast as the population. Yet teenage unemployment, almost 20 percent in 1975 (*World of Work Report,* 1977), still represents a large untapped labor pool likely to want part-time work.

HEALTH

Although health is by no means perfectly correlated with age, older persons often resist the long days in compressed workweeks more than do younger ones, presumably because of lower tolerance for fatigue. And as health problems of various kinds begin to surface, whether or not they are a function of increasing age, employee desire for schedules that accommodate health-care needs increases. Because of fatigue factors, revised career aspirations, lesser income needs, and tendency to be more reflective, persons over fifty-five probably become more interested in part-time work.

There is an increasing tendency for males from ages fifty-five to sixty-five to drop out of the work force. The drop-out rate has increased from 13.1 percent of the labor force in 1950 to 24.2 percent in 1975. A review of the age distribution of a local population, particularly in light of "the greying of America"—a steady increase in numbers of people over fifty-five—should present employers with opportunities to use this older group of workers more effectively.

GEOGRAPHIC LOCATION

Whether workers are in rural or urban areas seems to make a difference. Rural workers seem more satisfied with work that leaves urban workers relatively unhappy. One could hypothesize that they would also tend to favor compressed workweeks relatively more than their city counterparts, irrespective of age, because of the respectively different kinds of leisure time activities available and the lesser problems with daily traffic. Also, rural employees may farm or garden and prefer uninterrupted days during appropriate seasons, though they

Table 2.2

A Model of How Career Stages and Processes Are Connected to Life Stages,
Resulting in Variable Attitudes toward Desired Timing and Amount of Work

Age	Career Stages	Parallel Life Stages	Differential Effects of Life Stages on Men and Women in Regard to Time Availability and Desired Work Hours
1. 16–22	Exploration	Breaking out Experimentation with adulthood	Part-time work, odd jobs, odd hours (after school, vacations)
2. 22/23–28	Establishment stage	Establishing self in the adult world Single–working Marriage–children	Willingness to work long hours, over-time, not weekends or evenings. If single, or without children, the compressed workweek is attractive.
3. 28–33	Granting of tenure	Age 30—time of transition Occupational change and divorce Financial needs begin to increase	a) Men: Long hours, take work home b) Women: Drop out/part-time

Age	Career Stages	Parallel Life Stages	Differential Effects of Life Stages on Men and Women in Regard to Time Availability and Desired Work Hours

4. 30/33–40	*Maintenance*—mid-career	*Settling down*
		Youngest child leaves home to enter school
		Commitments deepen to work, family
			a) Men
			  1) If upward mobile, long hours, community work, flexibility
			  2) If plateau in work, regular hours /second job, attention to family
			b) Women: Back into career, part or full time, shared jobs, flexible hours desired

5. 40–45	*Maintenance*—late career	*Mid-life transition* Children leaving home to enter adult world *Reevaluation* and commitment to life-style, reordered priorities, *then* *Restabilization*, no children at home Wish for more enriching personal life—renewal of important relationships	a) Men: Steady hours not as long—longer vacations, weekends, education for renewal, either evenings or on sabbatical b) Women: Longer hours, perhaps flexibility. Health problems may begin to emerge requiring reduced hours.
6. 55–65	*Decline*	*Anticipation of retirement*	Men and Women: Tapering to part-time.

may prefer some free time every day in order to keep up with chores. Irrespective of geographic location, the availability of parking space may determine whether employees can take advantage of flexible working hours.

In one rural community, in the absence of public transportation or opportunities to carpool because of geographic disbursement, flexible working hours simply resulted in employees arriving increasingly early at work to compete for parking places. Many employees who preferred to arrive later were disgruntled; others simply resigned themselves to shifting to earlier start times. As a result, in that setting, flexible working hours did not fulfill its promise.

CONCLUSION

To predict preferences of persons for particular work schedules, career and life-cycle position should be tempered with other information, including nature of the work, employment of spouse, socioeconomic status, minority status, sex, education, health, and geographic location. When these factors are combined with the theoretical frames of reference that emerge from studies of career and adult life cycles, employers have a powerful tool for identifying potentially available manpower. The method can also be used to identify potential problem areas within an organization, or new scheduling arrangements to attract or keep desired employees.

The Institute of Social Research at Michigan, in a 1971 survey of workers' reactions to nineteen labor standards (Quinn and Sheppard, 1971), reports that 9 percent of all respondents had problems with "inconvenient schedules" compared to less than 1 percent, virtually none, in 1969. An increase in the divorce rate, in dual-job-holding families, in numbers of women in the work force (both married and independent heads of households), in numbers of teenagers seeking work, in changing values, and in the continuing shift of persons from the manufacturing to service sectors all contribute to the need for different work schedules at different times in peoples' lives.

Table 2.2, though by no means complete, combines selected circumstances with career and life-cycle concepts to indicate the likely responses to various scheduling alternatives. This information will be useful when using the concepts in Chapter 6 to relate employee needs to organizational requirements in order to derive suitable schedules.

3
FLEXIBLE WORKING HOURS

We use flexible working hours because it is consistent with our philosophy of giving employees the maximum amount of choice. They choose their hours just as they can choose their vacation time or the color to paint their machine—within constraints, with as much individual choice as possible. (Roger Hetherman, Director of Employee and Community Relations, Kingsbury Machine Tool)

I'm divorced with one child, ten years old. Flextime lets me come in early so I can be home when my daughter gets out of school. Before I would fight traffic to get home late in the afternoon. Then I would rush through dinner. By the time we were cleaned up I was pooped, couldn't listen or talk to my daughter, was often irritable, couldn't relax, couldn't help her with her school work. Now she's happier, I'm happier and her grades have improved tremendously. (File Clerk, Social Security Administration, Washington, D.C.)

WHAT IT IS

Flexible working hours is essentially a work schedule that gives employees daily choice in the timing between work and nonwork activities. Thus, more than other organizational arrangements, it treats an individual as a whole person, with a life outside work as well as in the organization. It is this characteristic of choice that distinguishes flexible working hours from all other work schedules. Because choice is its essence, it is not mutually exclusive of but can be combined with the other alternatives described in this book.

HOW IT WORKS

Under flexible working hours, special consideration is given to *band width*, or maximum length of the working day. In order to provide opportunities for flexibility, the band is usually extended, perhaps to twelve or sixteen hours per day rather than the customary eight or ten. This extended band is generally divided into *core time* and *flexible time*. Core time represents those hours when everyone has to be in attendance. Flexible time, sometimes called *flexitime* or *flextime*, represents the hours within which employees can decide for themselves when to be present. Employees who come and go during flexible time periods are often said to be *flexing*.

Though common core times are 10:00 A.M. to 12:00 noon and 1:30 to 3:30 P.M., they may be minimal, as little as one hour in a day, or not even required. Each working unit in an organization must have its own designation, based on an evaluation of its own needs and the needs of the organization. In general, the less interdependence among persons, and the more persons there are in a working unit, the less need there is for core times.

Figure 3.1 illustrates two of the many possible eight-hour workday patterns for a company with core and flexible times distributed as shown over a band width extending from 6:30 A.M. to 5:30 P.M.

Flexibility is limited by the number of *contracted hours*, which must be worked in a *reporting period*. Although reporting periods theoretically may be quite lengthy, they are commonly a day, a week, or a month. In the United States, contracted hours are usually seven to eight in one day or thirty-five to forty in one week. In Europe, where pay by the month is common, workers may contract for 160 to 180 hours in a month. An employee who contracts for forty hours in a week, with a core time of four hours in any one day, may vary his or her starting hours and leaving hours each day within the flexible time periods as he or she chooses, so long as forty hours are worked by the end of the week. Thus that person might work four hours on one day,

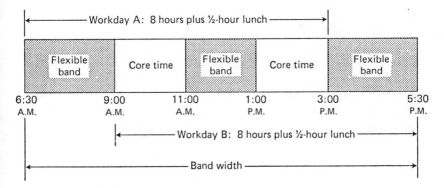

Fig. 3.1 Two possible workday variations under flexible hours.

and twelve on another, so long as the longer hours in one day can be accommodated within the band width.

Some organizations allow a *carry-forward* of *debit hours* or *credit hours*. Credit hours are hours worked in excess of the contracted hours in the reporting period. Debit hours are contracted hours in the reporting period that have not been worked. A person in an organization with a carry-forward allowance of 2½ hours, plus or minus, for 37½ contracted hours in a one-week reporting period, might therefore owe the organization 2½ hours, or be owed them. The common experience is for workers to carry credit balances. Despite the fears of many supervisors, most people seem to prefer to work now, play later.

LEGAL CONSTRAINTS

In the United States, the reporting periods have been severely constrained by legal provisions requiring the payment of overtime. The Walsh-Healy, Public Contracts Act, and Davis and Bacon Act, which affect a large number of employees under contract to the United States government, require the payment of overtime for over eight hours of work in one day to employees directly involved in manufacturing of goods and services under the contract. This standard has, because of its pervasiveness, even become the rule for large numbers of employees and companies not directly subjected to the laws. The Fair Labor Standards Act, which requires the payment of overtime for forty hours of work in one week, applies, with minor exceptions, to the balance of the work force.

Though legislation has been introduced in Congress to overhaul the wage and hour laws that apply to government employees, there are no clear signs that sufficient support can be marshaled to ensure their passage. Increasing public awareness of the need for flexibility in coping with the life-style problems of this and coming generations may, however, provide the leverage needed to produce change.

TIME RECORDING

Time recording for pay purposes and for the purpose of assuring punctuality is generally required by most organizations. Usually provided by time clocks, it is often a hated symbol of authoritarian control. Experience with flexible working hours reveals the use of a variety of devices, ranging from traditional time clocks, to manual records maintained by the individual employee, to time-accumulating equipment that records total hours but not times of arrival or departure.

If an organization has a reporting period of a week or more, time accumulators make it much easier for employees to keep track of their debit and credit balances. The use of equipment may also yield greater management control over employee time.

VARIATIONS

The degree of choice allowed distinguishes the varieties of arrangements of flexible working hours from each other. Many have acquired names. One variation is the *floating day,* adopted by the Nestle Company in White Plains, and Hewlett-Packard.

The floating day provides a very limited degree of flexibility. Decisions on daily time of arrival are made in advance, usually changeable only on one or more week's notice. Since there is no carryover, times of arrival automatically determine times of departure. Thus a person on an eight-hour day who arrives at 9:00 A.M. leaves eight hours later.

A variation suggested by Willi Haller, an early proponent of flexible working hours and President of Interflex Datensysteme GmbH, a manufacturer of time-accumulating equipment, is *variable hours.*

Under variable hours individuals would work according to demands of the job, varying work hours according to load on a daily, weekly, monthly, or seasonal basis. Although not formally working under such a system, farmers the world over and academics can be said to labor on variable hours.

Staggered hours, commonly associated with flexibility, is not really a flexible working hours variant, though it is often assumed to be. It is instead a form of fixed hours, which involves assigning to blocks of workers, usually without their participation or choice, starting and stopping times that will even out peak loads. Companies have used this arrangement to avoid congestion at elevators. Cities, including New York and Ottawa, have encouraged companies to go on staggered hours to ease loads on subways, city streets, and highways. Though staggered hours can ease congestion and is a better system than fixed hours for everyone, it is not flexible and has few of the other benefits listed later.

Systems based on flexibility can emphasize company or individual control, ranging from very little choice, as with the floating day, to total flexibility, as with variable hours.

ESTIMATES OF USERS

There is no completely accurate measure of the number of companies and individuals using flexible working hours and its variations, but informed estimates range between seven and ten million people. There are evidently over five million people in Germany on flexible working hours, and a million in Switzerland. Over 20 percent of the German and as much as 40 percent of the Swiss labor force are on flexible working hours. In the United States there are at least 400,000 people on some form of flexible working hours; the federal government experiments alone account for some 180,000 people, and a few large companies like Control Data Corporation and Hewlett-Packard account for more than 20,000 each. Metropolitan Life has 15,000. The number of companies trying some form of flexible working hours has accelerated rapidly from less than 100 in 1973 to approximately 3,200 in 1977. Federal agencies with flexible-working-hour experiments or full-fledged programs include the Federal Highway Administration, the Environmental Protection Administration, the Federal Energy Administration, and the Federal Maritime Administration. The Social Security Administration has recently decided to put over 18,000 employees on flexible hours. Since the first flexible working hours program in the United States began only in 1973, these numbers represent extremely rapid growth. The pattern in the United States seems to have roughly followed the European model since its beginning in Germany in 1967. Applications tend to be made first with white-collar workers in banks, insurance companies, pharmaceutical companies, engineering companies, and government agencies.

Because of the extensive interdependence of manufacturing work and the tendency of employers to be less trusting of blue-collar workers, applications to blue-collar work are still relatively uncommon. However, there is interest in application to manufacturing. For instance, at Kingsbury Machine Tool in Keene, N.H., a job-shop manufacturer of machine tools, eight hundred employees on two shifts operate on a variety of flexible time arrangements. Berol Corporation has an assembly line, with buffer stocks to reduce interdependence, so that the pencil makers do not all have to be there at once (Nathan, 1977). Organizations that have adopted flexible working hours have almost never given them up. The many articles in the management literature (*Harvard Business Review, California Management Review, Business Week*), popular magazines (*Psychology Today, New York, Time*), and local newspapers throughout the United States, suggest the sustained high level of interest in the concept.

ADVANTAGES OF THE METHOD TO ORGANIZATIONS

There are many reasons why the idea has spread so rapidly, and the list of advantages is long. Flexible working hours appears to be one of those rare innovations valued highly by both employers and employees.

Flexible working hours seems to have important effects on short-term absenteeism. Under fixed hours, many individuals who face the prospect of being late decide it is too embarrassing to come in an hour or so after everyone else has arrived, so stay away for the day and say that they were sick. Especially for those variations of flexible working hours in which there is no necessary starting time each day, short-term absenteeism decreases dramatically as employees get used to the idea of flexibility. At Berol Corporation, for example, absenteeism decreased 50 percent (Morgan, 1977). Surprisingly, in some organizations there are even decreases in long-term absenteeism. Since long-term absenteeism is presumably related to sickness, it may be that allowing individuals more choice about how to balance nonwork with work activities leads to greater feelings of autonomy and either less illness or greater commitment to the job.

Tardiness, of course, is virtually eliminated in those systems where daily starting times may vary. Thus a nasty, irritating, and recurrent problem, especially for supervisors, is eliminated by thinking about worktime in a different way. It is parallel to the astronomers before Galileo, who assumed that the sun went around the earth and had to make increasingly complicated explanations about why the predicted path of the sun was not followed. When the model was reversed, the problem disappeared. In our own research we found a dramatic example of a problem with tardiness disappearing:

> A black woman at a Boston bank had been labeled "chronically tardy" by her boss, even though she was competent at her work. He was ready to fire her because of this constant source of aggravation. Coincidentally, the department began a flexible working hours experiment. After a few days, this woman, whom the boss thought was "not ready to join the modern industrial labor force because blacks don't get the right kind of discipline" started coming in half an hour earlier than her former starting time! She had a child whom she took to a day-care center; when work started at 9:00 and the day-care center opened at 8:30, she could not physically get from the center to the bank in time, so she was always a few minutes late. When she could come to work within a broad range of time, she was able to make alternative arrangements for her child, leaving him at a relative's, and arriving early at work without having to wait around for the starting time.

Another reported difference is in the area of employee turnover. It is believed that turnover drops for most employees because they stick with an organization in order to enjoy the benefits of flexible working hours. This advantage, of course, will gradually disappear once the practice is more widespread. For others, the opportunity to adjust personal work schedule with personal life may make it possible to work with less aggravation and therefore to develop greater commitment to the job and to the employing organization. Implementation of flexible working hours may also indicate a general interest in employees that they appreciate and associate with other commitment-building practices.

The organizational outcome in which there is the greatest interest is, of course, productivity. Unfortunately, because most installations have been in the white-collar area, hard measures of productivity are difficult to obtain. A very high percentage of organizations trying flexible working hours report impressionistically that at the least there is greater enthusiasm for work, though no change in productivity. In addition, employees seem more physically ready to get to work when they have been able to adjust their schedule to take care of personal matters or avoid heavy traffic. One German study concluded that employees took 18 percent less time to reach standard output when they had choice over hours.

In a number of instances, productivity increases of 4–8 percent have been documented where employees work on products that have relatively long start-up times or lengthy processing periods. For example, studies in two Swiss watch companies found increases of 4 percent and 5–7 percent. Assemblers of watches had previously lost worktime whenever they came to the end of the workday and had an unfinished watch. There was considerable time lost in putting parts away at night and in setting up for starting the next morning. Under flexible working hours, personnel continued to work until they finished the watch they were assembling (Elbing, Gadon, and Gordon, 1974). Similarly, employees in a large American pharmaceutical company would not hesitate to start an extra batch toward the end of the day if they could stay until the batch was completed (Golembiewski et al., 1974). A Canadian EDP department that worked round the clock under a system by which employees in all three shifts coordinated their flexible times with one another recorded a 6 percent increase in productivity over the first year of its flexible-working-hours operation. Pacific Gas and Electric calculated savings of $300,000 from its flexible-working-hours installation in an engineering department after an expenditure of some $50,000 for time-accumulating equipment, and cited a variety of reasons for the savings, including lower absenteeism, higher efficiency, and so forth.

Though productivity savings are sometimes calculable only indirectly, they are nevertheless reported as substantial. The Kingsbury Machine Tool Company found that in the department where flexible working hours was first installed, the number of "lost hours"—that is, hours not worked for reasons such as paid or unpaid absenteeism, tardiness, and so on—decreased from 8.4 percent to 3.8 percent, while the rest of the factory remained constant at 5.2 percent over the same three-month period. A bank put its credit department on flexible working hours; though loan volume increased 20 percent that year, the department added two employees rather than the four that had been budgeted for such an increase. With flexible working hours the work was more evenly distributed and employees were apparently more committed to their work.

Experiments with 580 people in Massachusetts State Government Agencies resulted in about one-fourth of participating employees *and* their supervisors reporting increased amounts of work. In one unit, the Massachusetts Rehabilitation Commission, actual cases processed increased 3–4 percent in units on flextime (Harbridge House, 1977). Similarly, over one-half of participating supervisors and employees at Metropolitan Life reported increases in productivity while almost none reported decreases (Schein, 1976).

Productivity can also be affected if the change to flexible working hours leads to improved work methods or managerial practices. We studied a large urban bank with severe problems in its typing pool:

> The typing pool was run by a female former military officer. For a long time management had known that she was not very good at handling people and had tried a number of supervisory training devices. Nothing had made any difference. Finally, in desperation, management decided to try installing flexible working hours. The supervisor's military experience had conditioned her to believe that she could not possibly trust any employee whom she wasn't watching continuously. Therefore, she had utilized strict and close supervision. Under flexible working hours, it was not possible for her to be present during the entire working day, so that she was forced to let some work go on without watching it directly. As she gradually discovered that employees were doing their work, even when she was not present, she began to spend less time watching and more time in the office planning. As a result of this change in management style, productivity in the typing pool increased 9½ percent over seven months, as measured by the number of lines typed. This amounted to a saving of approximately $2200 per month, and "saving" of another kind—the "untrainable" supervisor had been "trained."

In another bank we studied, young women worked on Cardex "tubs," in which they recorded credit information for incoming telephone credit checks. With their supervisor they devised a way to take advantage of flexible working hours. Incoming phone calls had previously started at 8:00 A.M. and continued to 5:00 P.M. As a result of their search for a new method, incoming calls were confined to the period from 10:00 A.M. to 4:00 P.M. Customers were notified. Not only did employees thereafter have flexible start times, but they were able to post credit information to their cards before 10:00 A.M. Credit information was thus more up to date as a lag in posting was reduced. Customers, employees, and the bank all benefited from this arrangement. The young women trained a clerk working nearby to cover for them at hours when they were not there, leading to a reduction in bottlenecks due to absences.

ADVANTAGES TO THE INDIVIDUAL

In numerous surveys, people on flexible working hours report a number of personal advantages. Flexible working hours was originally invented to deal with traffic problems at a plant in Germany. Since then, reduced commuting time has frequently been mentioned as an individual benefit; it not only offers the individual extra time for pursuing personal interests, but also may facilitate a reduction in aggravation due to traffic jams.

The time saved in commuting or the ability to shift working hours to suit personal needs leads to other personal benefits. Individuals can, and do, use the time to pursue educational goals, spend more time with families, follow leisure interests, do necessary shopping and other errands, arrange for child care, and so on. In some cases a shift in times of work can result in dramatic life changes. Here is an example from our research:

> Charlie is a supervisor in an urban bank. He worked from 9:00 to 5:00 for twenty years; it had never occurred to him that the complexities of his family life could be other than they were. At the end of each working day he would fight the traffic to get home, and then sink into a chair to read the newspaper in the brief time before dinner. With only a short time before dinner, he could somehow never get around to work on the boat he was building in his basement. After dinner, he often had to take his wife shopping, since she didn't drive and they only had the one car. This schedule meant that Charlie was often irritable when he was at home. He never seemed to be able to interest his children in the

boat building he so much loved whenever he could find the time for it. After the implementation of flexible working hours in his bank, he found that his assistant supervisor, who was young and single, preferred to come in later in the morning and then work later in the afternoon. Charlie was an early riser, anyway, and so began to come in at 7:30 in the morning in order to leave at 3:30 in the afternoon. Because he got home earlier, the family's one car was available to his daughter, who volunteered to take his wife shopping. Within a short time his boys, out of curiosity, joined him after work in building the boat. Because he would get a running start before dinner, he found that he often was quite willing and able to get back to it after dinner, where his boys would once again join him. The greater interaction around boat building with his sons led to more free and easy communication with them that, in turn, made him feel better about himself. Because his wife could get the shopping done before dinner in the evenings she was more relaxed and often either joined in the boat building or socialized with the men. Thus a simple change in working hours had profound and far-reaching effects on family relationships and communications.

While this example is more dramatic than most, it is illustrative of how the option for being flexible can provide opportunities for the individual to make appropriate trade-offs between work and nonwork concerns. The black woman mentioned earlier who was able to make alternative day-care arrangements for her son illustrates how women or men with small children needing care can adjust their work schedule to see their children off in the morning and/or be home to greet them at night. Young, single men and women may extend their lunch hour in order to do shopping while downtown or to meet friends.

Another man we interviewed found that with flexible working hours he was able to at last get involved in educational activities in the community and run for the School Board. Previously he had been prevented by his work hours from being able to attend early evening meetings; with the ability to plan his work around the meetings, he was able to successfully run for and actively participate in the School Board in his community.

Repeatedly in our interviews and in the work of others, individuals say that it makes them feel really good to be allowed to make choices for themselves about worktime. They feel more trusted by the company and feel treated more as adults. This results, we believe, in a generalized enhancement of self-concept. Whether or not this greater feeling of adult autonomy leads to greater productivity, we believe it is worthwhile in and of itself. Independence and autonomy are worthy characteristics for adult individuals.

ADVANTAGES TO SOCIETY

If flexible working hours indeed leads to greater feelings of autonomy and enhanced self-concept, that alone has value in a democratic society. But even if the stock of healthy, adult individuals is not actually increased, there are other social benefits from flexible working hours. The smoothing out of traffic flows can result in significant savings of gasoline, capital equipment, and accidents. In Winterthur, Switzerland, which has 60 percent of its working population on flexible working hours, the community was able to reduce its number of buses by ten because the peak load of public transportation had leveled out. The City of Baltimore, and the Golden Gate Bridge Authority in San Francisco, have been exploring the encouragement of flexible working hours for just that reason. The Port Authority of New York City has since 1970 encouraged staggered working hours for similar reasons. A lengthening out of arriving and departing traffic means reduced rush-hour traffic, less tie-up of bridges and other transportation modes, and can lead to great savings for the city (Nathan, 1977). As more people use flexible working hours or other variations of the standard workweek, peak demands for recreational facilities are likely to be smoothed out. This can result in much greater use of existing capacity and a reduction of the need for major capital expenditures.

DISADVANTAGES OF FLEXIBLE WORKING HOURS

For a few companies there may be disadvantages. Flexible working hours is likely to be hardest on first-line supervisors. Often they do not have highly developed managerial skills and rely on first-hand presence and observation to see that work is done. Flexible working hours, with its extension of the hours during which some employees may be present, forces supervisors to do more planning. It requires them to assess what an individual can be expected to accomplish during a day or week, to plan work in advance so that those who come in early or stay late will have something constructive to do, to plan for and arrange ample coverage for those hours of the day or week when employees are less inclined to choose to be present, and so on. Thus, for many supervisors, new skills are necessary. Unless they are provided, supervisors are likely to feel threatened and insecure. The supervisor who has never had the experience of trusting employees enough to let them work without first-hand supervision is unlikely to leap with joy at the prospect of having to rely on workers that he or she cannot watch. Thus organizations wishing to go on flexible working hours need to work closely with the supervisors that will have to implement it. It should be mentioned, however, that even supervisors who are uncomfortable with supervising employees on flexible hours usually like the personal opportunity to flex their own hours.

A second disadvantage for organizations concerns communications. It may be harder to find times to hold meetings that require everyone's presence. Thus more consideration again must be given to planning.

Like any change, flexible working hours calls for careful analysis of the way things are done. Though ultimately such analysis is likely to benefit any organization, working out all the details of hours, coverage, allowance for absences, sick leave, and so on can be costly and time consuming. Though flexible working hours has been extremely popular, there have been a few cases where improper preparation has led to tension and fewer benefits than could have been realized.

The need for some kind of record-keeping system may be a disadvantage. When all hours are fixed, elaborate systems are not necessary for keeping track of employees' coming and going, though those who have to line up to punch a time clock would probably feel otherwise. But with flexible working hours it is desirable to develop a system, whether paper and pencil or mechanical, for recording accumulating hours. The less flexible the variation, the less problem there is. There are companies that record time completely on the honor system, asking each individual to be certain about working the required number of hours, but this also has potential difficulties, including employee mistrust of one another.

We have seen in some organizations that flexible working hours can make overt, subtle differences in status or contribute to defective decision-making processes, as employees dispute the method for how Friday afternoon coverage will be determined. Does the person with seniority have to stay late to finish work, or does she or he have the choice? Does everyone have to rotate Friday afternoon coverage, or should the supervisor decide that the least senior members should? The interpersonal problems these questions reflect illustrate the need for conflict-resolving skills that supervisors may not have and probably did not require before.

Another disadvantage for companies is that with flexible working hours buildings must be open longer and therefore bills for lighting and heating may increase. This can be offset by providing longer service hours to customers. It also may be offset by other energy savings, such as lower gasoline consumption because of reduced traffic jams, but these offsetting savings may go to individuals rather than to the company.

DISADVANTAGES TO THE INDIVIDUAL

It is hard to see what disadvantages there are for individuals except for those who might be disturbed by fellow workers coming and going throughout the morning and afternoon. Some employees may be uncomfortable about the idea of having to make choices about issues such as arrival and departure time, which were fixed in the past, but those employees can usually continue to work the same hours as they always have.

We have seen that those in organizations who already have informally sanctioned flexibility—usually professionals such as engineers—can resent a formal system that makes them strictly accountable. Where they formerly could bend hours a bit as needed, without adding up hours worked, the recording requirements of a formally adopted system can create a *loss* of freedom. Similarly, higher status individuals or groups may feel a relative loss of status when others also have the privileges of flexibility available to them.

DISADVANTAGES TO SOCIETY

Insofar as keeping buildings open longer requires increased use of energy for light and heat, there may be an overall cost to the society (if not offset by energy saved through improved traffic flow). It is hard to see what other disadvantages there might be.

THE LIFE STAGES FOR WHICH
FLEXIBLE WORKING HOURS IS BEST ADAPTED

Because flexible working hours is a system that gives individuals a measure of control over their working hours, the range of those who can benefit from it is great.

For example, the system of flexible working hours also enhances other alternatives to the standard workweek. Combined with part-time work, schedules may be individually arranged to provide opportunities for work for people in school, for mothers with young children, and for older people who want to slow down or partially retire. Used with job sharing, it provides the working pair with the possibility of dividing the worktime in many different combinations. Combined with the compressed workweek, it gives persons more options in distributing their worktime over a long workday so that they can take care of personal needs that are otherwise neglected or take rest periods in order to reduce fatigue.

For working mothers, flexible working hours is a particular boon. It gives them the possibility of arranging child care, staying home to see children off in the morning, or getting home in time to greet them from school. Many mothers who might not otherwise be willing to take jobs can be and have been attracted to the labor force. Westinghouse, for example, installed flexible working hours at its nuclear center for eight hundred employees to make it easier for women to fit their workday to their other obligations (*Newsweek*, 1976).

Single individuals who lead an active night life may appreciate flexible working hours because it gives them the opportunity to sleep late.

Executives or those in managerial positions, in the stage of their careers where they are establishing themselves and are upwardly mobile, may see little benefit from flexible working hours in its formal implementation because they already enjoy a kind of flexibility—though it usually means flexibility to work much longer hours than the standard forty per week.

Workers heading toward retirement may appreciate flexible working hours as it allows them to adjust their schedules so that they can become involved in volunteer activities or hobbies that will carry them into retirement. For them, however, the ability to reduce the number of hours worked per week may be a more important variation of the standard workweek than flexible working hours.

Single parents would certainly be major beneficiaries, whether male or female, as flexible working hours would allow them to make necessary arrangements for children. And, of course, those who have no special need to flex working hours can continue to work on a regular, fixed schedule, as do many already under flexible working hours. It is a potent method with wide application to those at various stages in their life cycle.

4
THE COMPRESSED WORKWEEK:
"FULL TIME" IN LESS THAN FIVE DAYS

The [Monday–Thursday] plan did everything we hoped it would, plus a few surprise benefits we hadn't counted on . . . I hate to think what would happen to morale if we ever went off it. (Grant Doherty, Kyanize Paint Company [Raskin, 1975])

I have been able to take courses, build more physical exercise into my life, do volunteer work, spend time with an elderly parent, have time and energy to spend creatively; long live the four-day workweek! (John Hancock employee)

WHAT IT IS

The compressed week is a method for allowing a worker to accomplish "full-time" work in less than the standard five- (or more) day workweek. By extending the length of the workday beyond the standard eight hours, a full week's worth of working time can be finished within three to four and one half days, allowing for more than the usual two days off. The extended "weekend," however, may come on any of the days of the week, depending on the particular compressed schedule followed. It is a method that usually yields many more three-day blocks of time off from work per year than do other rearranged workweek methods.

HOW IT WORKS

The compressed week can be utilized in two differing ways: most commonly, the unit operates for five to seven days, more than eight hours a day (up to and including around-the-clock), but individual employees only work three to four and one half days per week; or an entire firm or unit can operate only four days per week, with all (or most) employees in attendance for all of the four days. Under the first arrangement, days off will vary among individuals in such a way that the optimum number of employees are at work on the busiest days or at busiest periods of the day.

When many people hear of the four-day week they think only of the second arrangement, with the firm closed three days a week. But that is an arrangement suitable only to a relatively few firms with peculiar demand patterns. More typical is the firm (or unit within a firm) that desires extended working hours for its people; it schedules individuals to work a standard number of full-time hours (usually thirty-five to forty-two a week) in less than five days, thereby increasing the length of each working day. By doing this, organizations that have identified the pattern of load on their services or equipment can alter scheduling to fit load better; for example, a retail store can extend the hours it is open to to the public, a manufacturing firm working round the clock can reduce the number of shift changes from three to two each day while remaining in continuous operation, or a firm can get reluctant employees to work on some Saturdays and Sundays and at the same time provide more concentrated time-off periods for them.

The essential trade-off under a compressed-week system is that the employee works longer daily hours for more days off. Once a firm decides to utilize that principle, many variations are possible, and have been put into practice, depending on the needs for having employees present at particular times.

VARIATIONS UTILIZED

The most typical compressed-week pattern is to work forty hours in four days, giving rise to the abbreviation 4/40. The simplest pattern on this schedule is a Monday–Thursday schedule from, say, 7:00 A.M. to 5:00 P.M. or 8:00 A.M. to 6:00 P.M. Often in the same firm, others

Table 4.1
Four-Employee Firm,
Typical 4/40 Pattern

	M	T	W	T	F
A	x	x	x	x	
B	x	x	x	x	
C		x	x	x	x
D		x	x	x	x

will work a Tuesday–Friday schedule with the same hours, allowing five-day operations with less staff present on Mondays and Fridays than on Tuesday through Thursday. An example of such a pattern is shown in Table 4.1.

Further complications allow for greater numbers of employees at peak hours or on peak days when these do not fall in midweek; for some retail firms, for example, prime demand falls on Thursday through Saturday (or Sunday in states that allow retail sales for "non-essentials"). Thus variations in the days or hours when work is required can be scheduled to fit demand.

Another form of demand variation arises from the nature of the manufacturing process used, or from inherent job requirements arising from the work's layout or distribution. The natural cycle of manufacturing may not fit into eight-hour shifts, for example, or drivers making deliveries may waste time, gas, and oil if they must return within eight hours. Again, in such situations the scheduling of employees may vary from a repeating four-day, the-same-days-every-week-for-all-employees pattern, and can be adjusted to fit the situation. Further variations arise when the operations of an organization require more than eight to twelve hours each day, or more than five days a week. Organizations that must be open round the clock, seven days a week, such as hospitals or continuous-process manufacturers, often need highly complex staffing patterns. For example, two companies that do not shut down because of their continuous process technologies, Ciba-Geigy and Eli Lilly, schedule individuals for work cycles alternating between three-day and four-day weeks respectively, during which each individual works in sequence, day and night shifts, weekdays and weekends. At the end of the twelve- or twenty-four-week cycle, the rotation begins again (Pryblek, 1974). Thus, each week the employee gets three or four days off at a time in return for working a longer shift, day or night, weekday or weekend—in addition to regular vacations. (Some firms do reduce the number of holidays given to those on the compressed week.)

Similarly, several large insurance companies, including Equitable, Royal Globe, Guardian, Metropolitan, and Prudential, in order to maximize use of their expensive computers, have put EDP employees on three-day weeks. The employee works a 12 or 12½ hour shift (the extra ½ hour being for communications with the other shift) 3 days a week, so that the computer center operates six days a week, twenty-four hours a day. Essentially a person works Monday-Tuesday-Wednesday or Thursday-Friday-Saturday, day or evening, with the remaining days off. In order to share the unpleasantness of evening or weekend work, however, employees usually rotate through the shifts. This can get quite complicated; Guardian Life, for example, uses a twenty-eight-day cycle in which employees get one, four, and seven days off between three-day work periods.

The three and four days a week can, of course, be 3½ or 4½ days, and can be combined with other arrangements as necessary. One overall company pattern may include four-day weeks for production workers on two ten-hour shifts per day, and a five-day, four-hour part-time shift in between for those who do maintenance, clean-up, or other coverage. And where there is only one shift per day, it is possible to combine flexible working hours with the compressed week, allowing start- and stop-time variations provided that a fixed total of hours is worked each day or week.

Finally, as should be clear, the total number of hours per week need not be forty; some firms were already on fewer than forty hours before switching to the four-day week and maintained the same total. Others, like John Hancock, reduced from 37½ to 36 hours for those who chose to go on a four-day schedule, approximately equalizing total hours over the year by adjusting holidays. They have been satisfied that the altered schedule resulted in no loss of productivity.

Regardless of total number of hours worked in the week, the trade-off of a longer day for fewer days-per-week worked is usually received best when the days off are consecutive rather than intermittent through the week. Thus most firms utilizing the compressed week have found that they need to schedule individual time with two or more consecutive days off each week in order to make the compression attractive to employees. As a consequence, scheduling flexibility for individuals is somewhat constrained, though with sufficient numbers of employees, overall staffing can be closely matched to the peaks and valleys of work demand.

ESTIMATE OF COMPANIES
AND INDIVIDUALS UTILIZING COMPRESSED WEEK

After a period of rapid growth from 1970 to 1973, the number of employees working some form of compressed week appears to have leveled off. In its annual survey of wage and salary workers, the Bureau of Labor Statistics reported that as of May 1976 there were about 750,000 employees working full time in less than five days, about the same number as in May 1975 and 100,000 more than in 1974. That is about 1 percent of all full-time nonfarm wage and salary employees (Bureau of Labor Statistics, 1977). Mid-1977 figures again will apparently show no increase (*New York Times*, 1977).

This figure of 750,000 is somewhat lower than the August 1976 estimate of one million employees in some 10,000 firms that was made by Riva Poor, who has closely followed compressed-week developments since their beginning in the United States (Raskin, 1976). The U.S. Comptroller General, however, also estimates one million people in 3,000 firms as of April 1976.

Many of the organizations on four-day weeks are small. John Hancock Insurance, however, has employees on the four-day week (as well as on flexible hours), and Medtronics, in Minneapolis, has most of its 3,100 employees on four 9½-hour days.

Though there are still numerous organizations experimenting with and adopting compressed-week variations, there is a 4–15 percent discontinuance rate, which apparently has about equalled new adoptions. (Poor (1973) estimates 4 percent, while Hedges (1973) estimates 5–15 percent discontinuance of compressed-week schedules.) A study by Harriet Goldberg Weinstein of the Wharton School found that fifteen of fifty-seven firms surveyed had discontinued compressed-week schedules. A Chrysler parts depot dropped its experiment with the four-day week after only two months. The 130 workers overwhelmingly voted against continuance, at least in part because of loss of other work and pay arrangements that accompanied the experiment. There was also some expression of negative reactions due to disruption of family life; union officials disagreed as to the importance of this factor (Feron, 1974). In the rest of this chapter we will explore the advantages and disadvantages of the method and identify those for whom it is likely to be attractive. That should prove helpful in estimating the benefits and preventing problems where implemented.

ADVANTAGES TO THE ORGANIZATION

Productivity

Many organizations have estimated that productivity has either increased with adoption of the compressed week or at least remained the same. When the cost of production start-up and shut-down is high, and shifts are not continuous, savings from a reduction in operating days from five to four can be considerable. Employee idle time may also be less when the schedule can be designed to fit peak demands. In some compressed-week installations, employees have opted for the elimination of breaks in exchange for a shortening of the longer workday. And, though the effect may wear off in time, there is some indication that employees who highly value the extra day off are willing to work harder in order to keep the compressed week as a "benefit."

Measuring productivity, of course, is never easy, and even in firms where it can be done the shift to the compressed week is often accompanied by other changes that make it hard to isolate the particular impact of the new work schedule. For example, Swerdloff (1975) reports that a machinery manufacturer estimated that output increased 25–30 percent after the introduction of the compressed week, with little growth in the number of employees. However, results were contaminated by the company's move to a new building with more work space, better layout, and better working conditions one month after the schedule change. Swerdloff also reports that in one firm out of the sixteen he studied, there was a decrease in productivity, and that still other firms could not measure the impact accurately.

Productivity can sometimes be increased by extending service hours. A schedule that allows the organization to remain open longer, or to remain open when there is strong latent demand, can result in greater productivity per employee hour worked. Sometimes supply of services at new times can increase overall demand for the services (though longer service hours may merely spread out the same demand). Whether the extended hours increase sales or enable greater responsiveness to those utilizing the organization's services, the effects can be positive. For those few organizations that can meet actual demands upon the organization within four work days, and close for three consecutive days, there can also be savings in heat, light, and other costs associated with being open on a fifth day.

Persons are sometimes willing to work undesirable shifts in exchange for extra days off, thus attracting skilled employees who would not otherwise be available. This has been the case with EDP (electronic data processing) departments that run on continuous shifts, producing increased returns on assets as well as better service. When an operation is capital intensive, greater machine utilization can lead to considerable savings.

In some instances, the change to a compressed week has produced a better match between work schedules and peak loads, thereby significantly reducing the premium costs of overtime.

Morale

Many organizations have reported higher morale among a high percentage of employees. Although there is something ironic about the fact that morale is higher on the job because people have more concentrated time away from it, there is no reason to conclude that trading concentrated time off for longer work days is morally worse (or better) than paying more money for work that is unattractive. The recent successful negotiation by the UAW for more nonwork days each year is in part a response to their members' interest in giving up money in exchange for more leisure time. Furthermore, time probably passes more quickly, thereby making the work itself seem more interesting, though unchanged in nature.

Absenteeism, Tardiness, Turnover

A number of firms have reported reduced absenteeism, tardiness, and turnover. The reduced absenteeism stems partly from the fact that a great deal of absenteeism occurs on Mondays or Fridays. The "Monday and Friday absentee" problem tends to disappear if the compressed week provides an extended weekend. Employees are also less likely to sacrifice the larger percentage of their pay represented by loss of one day's work out of three or four as opposed to one day's work out of five.

The effect on tardiness is mixed. It is likely that those with family responsibilities, or those for whom the extended hours do not fit natural body rhythms, will find that getting to work on time is a strain.

In many firms, turnover has been dramatically reduced; in fact the move to the compressed week was in part originally motivated by an attempt to attract or hold employees. In other firms there was no effect, or even an increase in turnover until those who did not like a compressed week sorted themselves out and found other jobs.

Image

Finally, there is the advantage of enhancing the organization's image. Because they are seen as progressive, early adopters of the compressed week may be more attractive to both potential employees and customers. Some firms have reaped large public relations harvests through newspaper, magazine, and TV coverage. It may well be that the motivation for adoption of the compressed week, as with many innovations, is as much for general image enhancement as for the direct benefit of the firm and its employees.

ADVANTAGES TO THE INDIVIDUAL

Leisure

The primary advantage for individuals is the aggregation of "weekend" time. For example, those on the four-day week who are given three consecutive days off experience a 50-percent increase in the length of their weekend time. There can be little doubt that for many nonwork activities, a third consecutive day off has more value than the same length of time interspersed throughout the week. Many activities such as medium-distance travel, time-consuming recreational activities such as boating, work on a house or vacation home, and education, are made more convenient or even possible by the aggregation of time off from work.

Here are some comments from our research with four-day-week employees at John Hancock:

> Because of the four-day week, I have found time to build my own home. By doing this I have saved $25,000.

> My rearranged work week has allowed me the opportunity to return to college after thirty years. My schedule permits me to go

from work directly to classes without any wasted time, and then I have an extra day off for studies.

The desire for vacation in blocks is widespread in the United States. During the 1960s the average number of vacation weeks per employed person increased from 1.3 to over 1.7 weeks, while for many long-service employees the length of vacation grew to four weeks or more. The legal rearrangement of national holidays in order to increase the number of three-day weekends beginning in 1971 is another manifestation of the interest in blocks of time off (Hedges, 1971).

Commuting

Employees also enjoy savings in the cost and time of travel through arrivals and departures that are before and after rush hours, and through the elimination of one day's travel. Fewer days away from home can also reduce the cost of meals and clothing. For some people the compressed week allows reduction in child-care expenses, though that depends on the kinds of arrangements a person with dependent children can make.

Family Relations

The compressed week provides opportunities to spend time differently with different family members. "One significant benefit mentioned by a number of employees with school-age children was that while formerly they had very little time alone with their wives, now they had at least one day and sometimes two, each week, at home with their wives while their children were in school. This has meant a change in their marital relationship" (Swerdloff, 1975).

More John Hancock employees:

The four-day week has been a boon to my husband and I. He is self-employed and travels frequently. I am now able to accompany him on short trips. Sort of short honeymoons, and after eighteen years we both feel this is necessary to building a relationship that will last eighteen more years.

I have a severely handicapped child who is home only on weekends. This has limited the types of activities we can take part in with our other children on weekends. With the day off during the week we are able to schedule family activities which we had never been able to take part in as a family before. (This) has had a highly positive effect on my entire family.

The demands of the compressed week on married couples, especially those with children, probably add one more force toward reduction of differentiation in husband and wife roles. If the extended day pushes the other spouse to do some of the things that were formerly done by the working spouse, then men are likely to do more meal preparation and child care while woman are likely to do more household repair activities. Whether this is good or bad for society has been debated and is answerable only by reference to values. To the extent that EEO laws support the equalization of opportunity for women in all areas, then the compressed week supports national social policy.

In the same vein, the compressed week allows more time for personal business of all kinds by making time available at hours when it is more convenient to schedule medical and other kinds of appointments. Some employees with chronic health problems or with dependents having such problems have stated they would otherwise be unable to get proper care without repeated absenteeism.

Additional Work Opportunities

As a final advantage, the compressed week provides more opportunities to employees with substantial financial need to moonlight or to work overtime on their days off. There is no doubt that within the economy there is a substantial minority of employees who choose to moonlight in order to save money for particular goals or to support families and other life needs. The general proportion of workers who hold more than one job has ranged between 4.5 and 5.7 percent for the fifteen years from 1955 to 1970 (Hayghe and Michelotti, 1971). Those persons on the compressed week, however, seem to average two to three times as much moonlighting as the general population. In one early study, about 20 percent of the men on a four-day week and 10 percent of the women held some form of second job (Poor, 1970). At John Hancock, however, only 4 percent on 4/36 said they added second jobs. Nevertheless, it is clear that the compressed week creates the opportunity for moonlighting for those who want or need it and must, therefore, be seen as desirable from their perspective. It is arguable whether the support of increased opportunities to moonlight is desirable social policy, since some have claimed that moonlighting takes jobs away from the unemployed. On the other hand, Kopp Michelotti (1975) has argued that "very few of the unemployed could or would take jobs held by moonlighters" because of the kinds of jobs involved, the hours worked, and the available earnings when compared to the desires and skills of the unemployed.

ADVANTAGES TO SOCIETY

Economic

Because some jobs do not pay enough to be fully supportive of individuals or families, they would go unfilled if employees with a primary source of income were not able to take them as second jobs. Moonlighting does, therefore, distribute needed skills more easily throughout the economy.

The availability of larger time blocks for leisure seems to lead toward greater spending on such things as boats, recreational vehicles, vacation homes, and the like. Between 85 and 95 percent of employees on the compressed week do use their extra time off for leisure in one form or another. Social philosophers can argue about whether spending on leisure is good for the soul, but it does have a stimulating effect on the economy.

Any increases in productivity, of course, would contribute directly to national wealth. Finally, there are energy savings to the extent that travel time to and from work is reduced and organizations close for an additional day, though in organizations that maintain the same total number of working days but extend hours, energy costs for heating and/or cooling will increase.

Quality of Life

From the national point of view, any system that increases morale at work, and creates at least the potential for raising satisfaction within the family, adds to the quality of life and increases greatly the likelihood of societal stability.

It is difficult to assess the impact on health of more concentrated time at work and larger blocks of leisure time. Arguments have been made both ways. Left to their own choice, a large percentage of persons who have been given the option do choose larger blocks of leisure time. At least it can be said that those who prefer the compressed week (a function of their life circumstances, we would argue) are getting what *they* think is better for them.

DISADVANTAGES TO THE ORGANIZATION

Most of the disadvantages to organizations are a function of adverse effects on employees at various levels in the organization. One of the key issues is fatigue. The early studies on fatigue and work are inconclusive, except for those who must change shifts weekly. Such rotation causes a variety of physical ailments (Pigors, 1944). For many employees the longer day is tiring, though a number of surveys also report that for a high percentage of employees this is not so. As might be expected, fatigue is found more often in older employees and in women with household responsibilities than in younger workers. Even younger workers, however, sometimes find the longer day fatiguing because they do not slow down their nighttime activities on working days. Fatigue is in part a function of the nature of the job and its technology, and where it appears may often be alleviated by changes in the technology.

From the company's point of view, fatigue alone is not the issue, but its effect on concentration, errors, quality of work, injuries, productivity, and the long-term health of valuable employees. If employee output slows down at the end of tiring days, or if the last day of each person's workweek is less productive, as on Friday afternoons on the standard five-day week, then there can be serious difficulties for the organization. While many people seem to find that a three-day concentration of leisure is enough to more than make up for whatever fatigue they feel with longer working days, there are unanswered questions about the long-term consequences of that pattern.

Scheduling problems are often greatly multiplied, requiring from management more scheduling expertise than conventional schedules. While this is a disadvantage from one point of view, it is exactly the careful attention to scheduling that can result in the advantages cited above, and the need for greater management attention should not alone be a deterrent to adoption of the compressed week. Skillful scheduling may help solve other problems such as bottlenecks, load balancing, or machine utilization, so that the skills are worth acquiring in their own right.

Scheduling problems also apply to supervisors. If supervisors work on a compressed-week schedule, they may not be available for various management meetings and communications. Often they find work piled up on their desks during their absence, creating tension on the first day back. If they do not work a compressed-week schedule, the overlapping shifts can lead to problems of continuity, style, communications, and so on. Similarly, key personnel in general, whether management or worker, may not always be available when needed, and without careful timing this can be annoying, if not harmful to operating effectiveness.

For those firms who attempt to operate on only a four-day basis, there can be shipping and receiving problems when outside suppliers work a five-day schedule. Firms have dealt with this difficulty by keeping a skeleton crew in the shipping and receiving department, or by "training" outside organizations to adapt to the new schedules.

Tardiness and absenteeism have sometimes been adversely affected. Some firms have experienced an increase in tardiness with the compressed-week schedule. Even when absenteeism does not go up, a person who is absent misses a greater percentage of the work-week than does a person absent for a day on the standard week.

Finally, there are some legal complications for firms wishing to go on a compressed-week schedule. In addition to the Walsh-Healey Act, which requires overtime to be paid for work after eight hours in one day when a firm has government contracts over $10,000, there are other federal and state laws that place constraints on work schedules. Some apply specifically to women, minors, and night workers. Many union agreements also call for overtime after eight hours a day, even when it is not required by federal or state law. While many states have granted exceptions to the laws in order to implement compressed-week schedules, a firm wishing to adopt one must invest time and energy attending to legal issues.

Although a few unions have been willing to go along with the experiments, most of them treat changes in established patterns of leisure, working hours, and overtime very gingerly. The Fair Labor Standards Act passed in 1938, which set the standard workweek at forty hours, has been a sacred trust to unions. A number of unions are now beginning to gear up for a drive toward the thirty-two-hour week, and though that may be a long way off they are not eager to support moves toward longer working days without an overall reduction in the standard workweek. Unions and workers in general balk at anything that sounds as if it might involve more work for the same pay, and there must be careful attention to perceptions of fairness in any schedule change. Though only 25 percent of all employees are unionized, union opposition to the compressed week remains an important stumbling block to its wider use. On the other hand, the North East Florida Building and Construction Trades Council recently signed a special contract with Davy Powergas that combines four-day weeks with no-strike clauses and a wage freeze in order to secure long-term employment. "The men like the idea [of the four-day week]. It gives them a long weekend, or if the weather causes them to miss a day, they can make it up on Friday and they're almost guaranteed forty hours a week" (*Wall Street Journal*, August 30, 1977).

DISADVANTAGES TO THE INDIVIDUAL

If there are dependents in the house, children, or older parents and/or a working spouse, the longer day can be a great problem. First there are difficulties in arranging for child care, meals, and so on; then there is the burden of household chores after a long day at work. Women in particular bear this strain, for they are the ones who usually have the "second job" at home, the care of the household. This strain can take its toll. For example, "at one manufacturing company 20 percent of the female work force quit when a 4/40 program was initiated, citing fatigue and overlong hours—especially when added to the chores they still had to face at home at the end of the day." (Cross, 1971) In another study conducted by Riva Poor, which she uses to boost the advantages of the compressed week, 38 percent of the female workers, mostly over age thirty, said they had problems in adjusting to a four-day week. The female workers under thirty had much less trouble adjusting to the four-day week and are comparable to the men in the sample in that respect. Though Poor does not give more demographic data, we can safely assume that a greater proportion of the women under thirty are either single or do not have children and can therefore adjust more easily to the longer day (Poor, 1970). A Canadian study reported that among the firms that discontinued the compressed week, prime reasons were the difficulty in recruiting young married mothers, keeping them on the job, and dealing with their complaints (Riddell, Stead, 1973).

There can be other adverse effects relating to family life. While for some people the chance to have uninterrupted time with spouse or children is highly desirable, for others an increase in family contact only leads to greater friction, greater demands for doing undesirable jobs around the house, or increased alienation. Even if family contacts are desirable, having one member on the compressed week can lead to irritating or difficult schedule conflicts among family members.

The extended day can also interfere with other evening activities during the workweek. While some leisure is best done in blocks, there are many other activities that are done best or are naturally scheduled in the evening after dinner. Those persons who work long hours can find it difficult to participate in a variety of community, social, or recreational activities that were previously accessible. Indeed, in one study, those workers opposed to a four-day schedule saw it as reducing leisure hours per day (Mahoney et al., 1975).

A minor problem (although for some people important) is less-frequent public transportation at the beginning and end of an extended workday. Some people do not like to travel in the dark. Thus, while there are many potential advantages to some individuals in the compressed week, for others the potential disadvantages are great.

DISADVANTAGES TO SOCIETY

It is apparent that the compressed week creates greater demand for leisure facilities. While compressed-week schedules can spread out the demand when people have Friday or Monday off, they thereby also increase it from Thursday evening to Tuesday morning, potentially creating an ecological strain on bodies of water and parks by keeping facilities in more constant use.

Insofar as the compressed week can accelerate family difficulties, it is a potential destabilizing force, though most employees who find it to be inconvenient are likely to change jobs or make adjustments in family living.

Finally, there has been considerable controversy concerning the ability of large numbers of persons to use large blocks of nonwork time wisely and constructively. Though there is some evidence that people who do boring work spend their leisure time in the least creative ways, it is our belief that individuals should have their own opportunity to structure their leisure activities. We doubt that there is serious danger to society from the creation of blocks of leisure time, even though some people may choose to "waste" that time by engaging in activities that some might think are not especially ennobling or self-actualizing. The arguments in the early 1900s against the five-day week, which was reduced from six days, have some of the same moralizing tone. Fear was expressed that employees with two days off per week would drink away the time (Sprague, 1973). It is always, of course, "others" who will fail to use the time wisely. A recent study comparing four-day and five-day workers found that the four-day employees used their leisure in about the same ways as they had before. They spent more time in child care and outdoor activities, not in watching television or carousing (Maklan, 1977). So fears seem misplaced.

LIFE STAGES THIS METHOD BEST ACCOMMODATES

As should be apparent from the previous discussion, the compressed week is least suitable for those who have small children, whether they are married or are independent heads of household. It is also less appropriate for older workers who are beginning to lose energy and stamina. And it is not likely to be well received by workers in rural areas who also farm, since farming requires daily activity, which, when added to long days, can create undue fatigue. Weinstein (1975) reports on a rural situation where the long days were compounded by fifth-day overtime, and employees complained, especially during the summer.

The compressed week is an ideal schedule for single people, those under thirty without children, and others in good physical health. It is also well suited to those in income brackets where a second job is necessary and where life circumstances allow for high numbers of hours to be worked each week by combining a first and second job, and to those jobs that do not require a high degree of physical exertion and/or that have natural resting periods. A machinist, for example, who has cycle time between set-ups that allows reduced attention while the machine is running, can probably work a longer day than the key-punch operator who must continually feed in data. Finally, those professionals who need creative, regenerative time may be especially well suited to compressed-week schedules, as they work intensively on projects and then have time away to allow unconscious processes to problem-solve or regenerate.

Because the compressed week is the most demanding of the altered work arrangements, it probably requires the most extensive thinking through before implementation, not only in terms of work flow, but also in terms of who the work force is and how the altered schedules will fit their life needs.

5
PERMANENT PART-TIME AND JOB SHARING

We realized several years ago it was stupid to cut off relations with good employees. Full-time Equitable employees can switch to part-time work after five years and enjoy a full range of fringe benefits. . . . Most so far have been women, mostly in the child-rearing years. (E. James Young, Vice-President, Equitable Life Insurance (Main, 1977))

I think that job sharing is fantastic. If I had to work full time I just couldn't give enough time to my year-old baby. This way I am a real part of the organization and have a chance for a full-time job when I'm ready. (Receptionist, Alza Corporation)

WHAT IT IS

Part-time work, in which the employee voluntarily works less than the prevailing standard number of hours per week, has always existed. But the concept of permanent part-time is relatively new, and less easily defined.

First of all, permanent part-time is not necessarily permanent from the point of view of the individual; it may well be more enduring than casual part-time work that lasts only for a season, but is often "temporary" in that it lasts only during a particular life phase such as raising small children. From the organization's point of view, however, permanent part-time positions may indeed be more permanent in that they are available indefinitely regardless of the tenure of the jobholder.

Furthermore, the concept of permanent part-time (PPT) as used in relation to altered work schedules connotes some kind of career-relatedness with potential for upward mobility that has not in the past usually been associated with part-time work. And while PPT can be established without mobility implied or likely, its attraction in recent years has been the possibility of enfolding PPT into a long-term working career.

At the same time, many who cannot or will not work full time are benefited by the availability of part-time work, even when it is not a direct part of a career ladder. So we will not totally ignore "regular" part-time work in looking at alternatives to the standard workweek.

Job sharing is a particular kind of part-time work in which one full-time job is divided by two people, each of whom works an agreed-on portion of the job. There are several variations possible: each works a half-day, with or without overlapping hours; each works a half-week; the week (or month) is divided unequally by mutual agreement; each is responsible for the whole job even though working part-time; each is responsible for half (or another proportion) of the job according to skills or job needs, and so on.

The two parties in job sharing need not know one another prior to starting the job, though a number of such arrangements involve husband and wife or good friends, but for more complex jobs they will have to communicate openly at least about job-related issues in order to see that each can do his or her share. For less complicated jobs, or for those that divide clearly, either temporally or geographically, each partner may work independently.

HOW IT WORKS

PPT can be used in a variety of ways. It can be a shortened daily schedule aimed at mothers of children in school, from approximately 9:30 A.M. to 2:30 P.M. With such an arrangement, either work is assigned that can be completed within that period, or another shift follows, full or part-time. For example, Massachusetts Mutual has a 9:30 A.M. to 2:30 P.M. shift, called "mother's hours," followed by a short three-hour shift for high-schoolers to continue the clerical or programming work.

Another way of using PPT is in an odd-hours shift. Organizations that wish to extend service hours might have a shift that works 5 P.M. to 9 P.M. daily. Others might augment employee numbers to cover busy hours during the regular workday or workweek. Many service organizations, especially those serving food, have peak hours when much more help is needed than at other times.

PPT has also been combined with the compressed week, as noted in Chapter 4, to provide a swing shift between two ten-hour shifts, allowing organizations to stay open around the clock yet still offer attractive workweeks. Employees can agree to work some minimum number of hours and be on call for more, or can work a fixed number of hours but at mutually convenient times. In either case, PPT would have the added benefit to organizations of enabling them to adjust timing to work demands, and to individuals of enabling them to balance nonwork with work activities.

Job sharing works in comparable ways. Usually the most effective arrangements are those in which the people sharing a job feel joint and complete responsibility for it, regardless of which one is present. Here is a description from *Peninsula Magazine* (Bagchi, 1976) of one shared job that is working well:

> Elwood Pierce admits he was skeptical at first. "Chris's qualifications were impressive," he says, "but he really threw me a bombshell when he said he would only work part-time."
>
> Pierce, director of operations for the School of Medicine at Stanford University, recently interviewed several candidates for the full-time job of facilities coordinator of the new Sherman-Fairchild Neurosciences Center. After some deliberation, he hired two coordinators—Chris Jackson and Pat Cross. . . .
>
> The position called for a wide variety of experience; someone able to consult with faculty regarding the ordering of special scientific equipment and someone knowledgeable in the installation and use of such equipment. Ms. Cross's prior work experience was in research and teaching, while Jackson is an engineer.
>
> "What we had together added up to an almost perfect package," says Jackson.

Indeed, this is what finally sold Elwood Pierce on hiring them as a pair. "I was really impressed with the fact that the two of them as a team had a stronger background than any single one of the candidates I talked to. . . ."

"Good communication is essential," he says. "If Chris is gone and someone should call about a project he is working on, Pat will need to know the answers—and vice versa."

Cross and Jackson are aware of this. They make a point of consulting one another often, and, in fact, enjoy the mutual support they receive. Both agree that "there is a real spirit of cooperation between us."

Currently they are dividing up their time and responsibilities to best meet the demands of the job. They plan to vary their hours (with some overlap time daily) and anticipate Cross's involvement will be largely in ordering the right types of scientific equipment and Jackson's will be in the proper installation.

Why did they choose to share one job? Pat Cross says she wanted to spend more time at home. "I'm a single parent, and now that I'm not working all day, I have more time to be with my child." She talks about having more time for outside interests, too, which include playing the flute and renovating an old home.

Chris, on the other hand, sees job sharing as a temporary way to meet his present financial needs. "I work part time in another department at Stanford," he says, "and this job helps to supplement my income."

So far, Elwood Pierce is pleased with the situation and offers his advice to other employers who might be considering it. "Get the right combination of people," he says, "then talk to someone who has given it a try to find out what their experiences have been."

One of the key aspects to PPT is the way in which fringe benefits are handled. Some part-time employees get no benefits at all other than those mandated by law, such as social security. About one-half to three-fourths of employers provide proportional compensatory benefits to part-timers, such as paid vacations and holidays. The part-time employee accumulates these benefits in proportion to actual time worked. Less than one-half of employers provide to part-timers any supplemental benefits, such as pension, life insurance, health insurance, and so on.

PPT and job sharing, however, are usually discussed as implying that *all* benefits should be prorated to hours worked. Since exact prorating would slightly increase costs to employers due to the way social security and unemployment compensation are calculated on a per person basis, Catalyst (1975) has proposed that the increased cost of these benefits for part-timers be subtracted first from all other benefits, so that PPT and job sharing will cost no more to employers in benefits. Without prorated benefits, PPT causes disproportionately greater income losses than mere reduction of hours, and is that much less attractive to individuals.

ORGANIZATIONS AND INDIVIDUALS USING PPT

Part-time work has been thought of largely as work for women and the very young. There are actually a large number of others who are interested in or currently doing part-time work. These include:

- Those who are nearing retirement and want to taper off

- Those who are retired but still wish to remain active

- Those in high school or college who need extra income or want to explore the world of work*

- Those who are seeking further education or retraining and wish to continue working while doing so*

- The handicapped who can work but cannot sustain full energy for full-time work

- Those who have reached a career plateau, have a decreasing interest in work, and no longer need full income because children are grown up.

---

* Part-time work under these circumstances has a temporary quality, sometimes for the individuals involved, as with the high school example, or for the organization, or for both, as was the case for the New York Telephone Company. Though part-time of a temporary nature is an important alternative that creates special opportunities for work, it is distinctly different from permanent part-time work.

- Those who are working but desire or need a second job (moon-lighting)

- Those who would otherwise be laid off during periods of recession* (for example, New York telephone reduced 2,000 of their 5,800 telephone operators to four-fifths time so that they would not have to lay off 400 recently hired women and minority people)

- Men who are family oriented and want to spend more time at home with their children

- Anyone who has sufficient outside interests and low enough economic needs to choose not to work full time.

Many of those on this extended list can be valuable and dedicated employees who would otherwise not be able to work at all, or would give less than their whole-hearted commitment to work that demands more hours than they are able or willing to give.

Because of the difficulties in creating a precise definition of part-time work, all quantitative estimates are slightly arbitrary. The U.S. Bureau of Labor Statistics defines part-time employment as less than thirty-five hours per week but does not distinguish between the varying kinds of part-time work. In 1974, 20.8 percent of those who worked in the United States worked less than thirty-five hours per week. Thus, over fourteen million people are working less than full hours. Of those working part-time, some 80 percent of those in non-agricultural industries were doing so voluntarily, and not because they could not obtain full-time work or had been cut back in hours by their employers. Nollen et al. (1976), in their excellent and comprehensive review of permanent part-time employment, make an estimate that 59 percent of all part-time employment is permanent. They base this on the number of those working part-time who have worked for more than half a year on part-time. By far the greatest percentage of part-time workers among males are eighteen to nineteen (44 percent) or over sixty-five (44.5 percent). Only 2.2 percent of males thirty-five to forty-four years old work part-time. Thus a high percentage of males are probably not working permanent part-time in any career-related way. Overall, only 12.3 percent of males work part-time, while just about one-third of all working females work part-time. And even in the prime age ranges between thirty-five and fifty-nine, at least one-fourth of women who are working, work part-time.

Similarly, only 5 percent of married men are working part-time, while 28 percent of single men do, yet 28 percent of married women, 21 percent of divorced, widowed, or separated women, and 24 percent of single women work part-time. Thus it is reasonable to infer that very few men relative to women are working in career-related part-time jobs. And since a very high proportion of all part-time jobs are in wholesale-retail trade or service industries and are lower skilled, the actual number of employees who work permanent part-time as a way of keeping up with their careers is undoubtedly considerably smaller than the total of those who work part-time for more than half a year.

Nevertheless, a significant number of males and females in the technical/professional area voluntarily work on a part-time basis. For example, 5.5 percent of all males and 19.4 percent of females working in technical and professional jobs voluntarily work part-time. Few people in managerial jobs, however, work part-time although there have been a handful of experiments with part-time managers that worked out quite well (Greenwald, 1973). While managerial jobs theoretically could be performed on a part-time basis, there are many pressures making this unlikely. Not only is it harder to segregate portions of the managerial job into time-bounded segments, but there are powerful norms in many organizations about managerial availability and lengthy hours, which would put the part-time manager at a serious disadvantage in terms of the access to information through informal relationships, which is necessary to be effective.

A manager is so overburdened with obligations that he cannot delegate his tasks. As a result, he is driven to overwork and is forced to do many tasks superficially. (Mintzberg, 1975)

There are some reports, however, of successful part-time employment in managerial occupations, especially in deliberate programs. (Nollen et al., 1976 citing Silverberg, 1972; Bronson, 1972; Meredith 1960; Darrow and Stokes, 1973).

Many technical and professional jobs, on the other hand, can indeed be time-bounded by project or by number of clients to be served. A female doctor, for example, such as the one working at the Newmarket, New Hampshire, Health Center, can choose to work a limited number of hours per week with no loss to the organization since patients are not scheduled when the doctor is not going to be there. And by working part-time, even while raising children, the doctor is able to maintain crucial skills, keep knowledge current, and remain professionally stimulated.

Most part-time jobs, however, have in the past been limited to low-level service and clerical jobs. Only recently, because of interest in providing career-related opportunities especially for women, have more jobs been opening up on a part-time basis at higher levels of salary, skill, and responsibility. For example, the Department of Health, Education, and Welfare began a pilot project in 1971 for twenty-two women to promote opportunities for those who would not or could not work full time. Similarly, the Department of Housing and Urban Development ran an experiment from 1967 to 1971, beginning with eight people who were hired part-time for jobs where there was not full-time work available. HUD now has a crew of one hundered permanent part-time positions where employees work up to thirty-two hours per week. This is the largest group in any federal agency and there is a long waiting list of people who would like to get into the crew.

The Veterans Administration, the Atomic Energy Commission, and the Social Security Administration have all had comparable experiments and there has been an increase in each of the last three years in the numbers of permanent part-time positions in the federal government. Recently the Civil Service Commission has encouraged using part-time employees for professional and technical positions, as the experiences in those agencies that have been using part-timers have been overwhelmingly positive (Comptroller General, 1976). Of the employees of the executive branch of the government, 8 percent, or 225,000, are part-time, and 7.3 percent of the total federal work force is on part-time.

The U. S. Post Office is the largest government employer of those on permanent part-time, employing 60 percent of all those on PPT in 1973. About 27,000 nonpostal government employees are working permanent part-time (U.S. Civil Service Commission, 1974). Of those who are part-time in the government, half the men and almost 90 percent of the women are nonprofessionals, and most of those who are professionals are in the health field. Four times as many men as women are in the higher grades of government service, GS-11 or above (Eyde, 1975). Senator Tunney has proposed a bill mandating that 10 percent of all government jobs up to GS-16 be reserved for part-time workers, but so far it has not passed. However, similar bills have been passed in Massachusetts and Maryland for state employees.

State governments also have their share of part-time employees. New York State alone has 6,800 positions that are part-time and multifilled, that is, actually shared by two or more people (Temporary State Commission, 1976).

The experiment generating the most interest in permanent part-time workers was carried out in Framingham, Massachusetts on the initiative of Catalyst, an organization devoted to helping women with career opportunities. In that experiment, fifty social workers were hired half-time; researchers found that the part-timers carried considerably more than 50 percent of the case load of full-time workers, and had more face-to-face contact with clients with only one-third of the turnover rate (Catalyst, 1971).

Many companies use part-time work in general, and an increasing number have been using permanent part-time to foster career opportunities. A prominent example is Massachusetts Mutual, with its "mother's hours" from 9:30 A.M. to 2:30 P.M. Metropolitan Life has 150 employees who work alternate weeks. Lockheed, Hewlett Packard, AMPEX, United Air Lines, Alza Corporation, New York Telephone, American Institute of Research, and the Stanford Research Institute are other private organizations using some form of permanent part-time work. Barclay's Bank in England has over one thousand employees who share jobs and child care in pairs.

Many of the arrangements for job sharing have been created in public school systems, libraries, and other educational institutions. MIT, Grinnell College, Scripps College, and Oberlin College have all hired husband-and-wife teams for one position. More than nine districts in the San Francisco Bay area have job sharing for some one hundred teachers, librarians, and media and resource coordinators. The Madison, Wisconsin school system has some shared teaching jobs. There are 120 pairs of teachers sharing jobs in the Framingham, Massachusetts area, and the U.S. Department of Education found 300 superintendants who had used part-time teachers and were overwhelmingly favorable about their experiences (Catalyst, 1971). The city of Palo Alto has twelve shared positions. As yet there are only a few companies with job sharing in existence, though there appears to be increasing interest.

In general, those organizations that have used part-time as a conscious employment tool are much more favorable about it than those organizations that have never tried it. Managers fear the complexities and costs of part-time work or job sharing when they have no experience with it, but do not find it as complicated in practice when they have actually had experience with it.

ADVANTAGES OF PERMANENT PART-TIME AND JOB SHARING TO THE ORGANIZATION

Though there has been little hard research done on organizational benefits from using PPT, there is considerable anecdotal evidence that there are a number of organizational advantages. Part-time can lead to reduced overtime payments, turnover, absenteeism, and time lost for breaks during work. The experiment in Massachusetts with social workers, for example, reduced turnover to a third of that of full-time employees. Turnover may be less because of great appreciation by part-time employees for the opportunity to work at all, because of the ease with which individuals working part-time can manage their personal lives, or because job frustrations are lower when a person is not faced with them on a full-time basis.

Availability of Employees

A related organizational advantage is that the use of PPT often attracts talented people who might not otherwise be available for work. In areas where there are general labor shortages, part-time can often tap labor pools not able or willing to work full time, and/or retain employees who want to go off full time, but do not want to stop working. For example, Ashland Oil in Ashland, Kentucky found it difficult to hire sufficient numbers of clerical and secretarial employees because of the rural location and outmigration of young people. About five or six years ago the company realized that the wives of present employees were a large untapped group of potential employees. Many of the wives did not have the economic need to work, but were interested in doing so, at least in part, because Ashland provides fewer outside activities than do large cities. They represented a wide range of skills, and ranged from those who were totally untrained and could do clerical work to those with legal secretarial background.

What started as a small program is now widely utilized and accepted, to both the company's and the wives' benefit. As the children of some of the employees have grown up, the mothers have moved to full time, while others prefer to stay part-time. In many cases hours are set mutually by the supervisor and the woman to adjust to life and work needs. At first the wives who were employed were seen as temporary fill-ins for full-time employees who were sick or on vacation, but the labor shortage in that particular area led to making the part-time arangements more permanent.

Though there has been widespread unemployment for the last several years in the American economy, there are shortages in particular job categories and in particular locations. Massachusetts Mutual's "mother's hours" helped to create a large applicant pool of people willing to assume routine entry-level jobs, and to perform in them with greater than average productivity. Permanent part-time work or job sharing can often be a way to utilize someone with a particular talent who would not work full time but is willing to give some time. Much of the use of permanent part-time in Europe, for example, is a result of widespread labor and/or skill shortages.

Organizations have found that those who work part-time in the beginning often become more interested in working full time for the organization at a future date. Thus PPT can be an excellent recruiting source, as it also allows the company to observe the person at work. At the same time, it creates opportunities for minorities and students, who can gain exposure to the world of work and become interested in the particular organization. This can be very useful to organizations, not only in finding untapped sources of employees but also in meeting Affirmative Action goals and EEOC guidelines; part-time employees are counted the same as full-time employees in estimating percentages of women and minorities at work.

Timing

Another advantage of PPT is that it allows for greater flexibility in staffing to meet actual demands. Not only can part-time workers be used to avoid paying time and one-half or double time for overtime, but they can also be scheduled to augment the work force during peak times and emergencies, special projects, and so on. They can also be used to extend service hours to the public, which is increasingly important in an economy that is already more service than manufacturing. And since we are steadily becoming even more of a service economy, the need for flexibility of employee times will be even greater, and permanent part-time and job sharing can be very useful in meeting these needs.

For example, duPont wanted to expand operations at its Athens, Georgia fiber-packaging plant to weekends. When full-time employees did not want to work weekends, duPont hired part-timers, mostly students. While they don't develop as much dexterity as regular workers, the part-timers have proven satisfactory, and over two hundred have been hired (*Wall Street Journal*, August 23, 1977).

Similarly, in industries that have extensive capital equipment, it is possible to use PPT to extend shifts so that the equipment is in more constant use. This is comparable to the use of the compressed work-week for maximizing capital equipment use, but may require less extensive rescheduling of full-time employees.

Permanent part-time can also lead to better service to customers, or to decreasing backlogs, because employees can be scheduled to eliminate logjams where there are insufficient full-timers to meet demands.

Productivity

There is considerable evidence that permanent part-time employees and those in job sharing are at least as productive as full-time employees and often even more so. In an industrial survey by the American Society for Personnel Administrators, 122 companies reported that part-time employees had higher productivity than full-timers. At the Social Security Administration, part-timers are also more productive than regular employees, possibly because of fears of being the first to be fired if they are not productive, since they have low priority in the federal personnel manual. Nollen et al. (1976) cited a number of studies demonstrating that part-time workers produced proportionately more than full-time workers. Employees on part-time often work at a faster than standard pace, because they don't get fatigued in the shorter period. When they are assigned to do tedious work they will often take it in stride better than full-time employees. The use of part-time employees may make it possible to reorganize the work of full-time employees to foster their working at full capacity, because the part-time employees can be given some of the less demanding tasks. But even where permanent part-time employees are working at complicated, professional work, such as the social workers cited in the Catalyst study mentioned earlier (1971), they were often proportionately more productive than full-time employees.

The Control Data Corporation set up a bindery in the ghetto of St. Paul, employing on a part-time basis mothers with children in school, the handicapped, and students. Among other things, they found that productivity at this plant was among the highest within the corporation, and they have been very pleased with its results. (For more details on this operation, see Chapter 6.)

Permanent part-time also creates the possibility of using part-time help for jobs that do not really require a full-time person but still require completion. Actual work needs can be matched to work hours, reducing requirements for overtime. Those on part-time tend to take fewer breaks and are willing to work more continuously than those on full time.

Another form of increased productivity often comes with job sharing. As one school principal remarked about teachers who share jobs, "Job sharing often means paying for two half-time workers but getting about two-thirds time from each person." Especially with professionals, or those doing technical work, where the individual is likely to have a certain professional pride in doing a job well, each party is likely to do even more than is required in terms of hours in order to make sure that the job is done properly.

Alza Corporation has had positive results from its experiments with job sharing in nonprofessional jobs. It has three pairs of receptionists' jobs that are shared by women with small children. The personnel department reports that they are very enthusiastic about the performance of all the pairs; when the members of one pair left to continue their education, the department that employed them insisted on filling the position with another job-sharing pair. The receptionists also handle logs and participate as members of their departments; most important, they take their jobs very seriously and do more than is usual for people in such jobs. Rita Williams of Alza's personnel department reports that:

> there's an advantage to having two people do that job, because it's not very exciting and each can give more energy when working only four hours per day. They don't poop out in the afternoon and their interest level stays higher. Furthermore, when one is on vacation or sick, the other fills in, which is an advantage because we get competent coverage; a temporary person can't be

instantly trained to do the job. We find that the women sharing the jobs voluntarily spend five or ten minutes together daily communicating with one another about what has happened when the other isn't there. Though we started with lower-level jobs, we can envision any job being shared as long as the supervisor wants it.

Similarly, the Assistant Director of the Winchester, Massachusetts Public Library reported that shared jobs for both professional and support staff had led to better service (*Library Journal*, 1976).

Another advantage of job sharing is that older workers can share their knowledge before retiring by teaming up with a less experienced employee for some period of time:

A chemist in a food-processing plant wanted to return to school part-time to work toward an advanced degree. She arranged to share her job with an assembly line worker and trained the younger woman as her technician. The resulting restructured position allowed her time to return to school and enabled the newly trained technical assistant to learn a new job skill. (Cunningham, 1976).

In short, there are many advantages to organizations in using PPT work and job sharing.

ADVANTAGES TO INDIVIDUALS

The primary advantage of permanent part-time work or job sharing to individuals is, of course, that it allows them to manage both a career and demands at home. Hoffman and Nye (1974) found that part-time work was particularly good for both women's and children's psychological health and even had positive effects on marital satisfaction. While women's organizations have been in the forefront of pushing for PPT work and job sharing, in order to allow women to raise families and yet not lose total touch with their career interests and training, there are many others who also can and do benefit from part-time opportunities.

When women interrupt their work for childrearing, they lose experience and seniority, which often leads to lower wages and earning capacity. Even now in the United States, working women average only 58 percent of the pay of working men. While the discrepancy is due partly to direct discrimination, it is also a reflection of the fact that high numbers of women temporarily drop out of the labor market for childrearing and fall behind those working full time and continuously. They find it difficult to make up what they have lost. Thus, PPT work and job sharing are an enormous help in keeping such individuals from acquiring a time handicap they cannot overcome.

Those who have had the opportunity to work part-time or in job sharing are often extremely enthusiastic. Note these comments from a group of teachers who participated in job-sharing experiments in the San Francisco Bay Area:

> There is no way the children in my class could have as good a program in art, science, or music if I were not sharing my job with Liz. (A single parent)

> I'd have preferred giving up my right arm to giving up teaching altogether after nineteen years. (Teacher under doctor's orders to slow down or quit)

> If I had to go back to full time I would have had to drop grad school. (Teacher getting Master's degree in early childhood education)

> It's the best of both worlds—a professional job, stamina, and time for my family. (*New Ways to Work,* 1976)

Above and beyond those who have to work part-time, individuals with strong interests besides work can find exciting and meaningful arrangements through PPT or job sharing. For example, Bill Leland, sharing a job as codirector of the Action Research liaison office at Stanford University, maintains that "there is no one full-time job that can satisfy everything in my life." He likes being able to spend more time than in his previous jobs at home with his family.

Some young couples are experimenting with each partner working part-time so that both may share in childrearing and in pursuing other interests. One such couple is Sheila and Ryan Mulcahy. Sheila works part-time at the Extension Division of the University of Wisconsin while her husband, trained in theology, is currently doing a variety of jobs leading toward permanent part-time radio work. Because they are ardent advocates of the life-style they have chosen and are articulate about its advantages to them, we include extensive comments from Sheila:

I'm a part-time employee of the University of Wisconsin–Extension academic staff. I do a full-time job thirty hours a week. I've also worked twenty hours a week and forty hours a week at this same job. I've had much experience with part-time, full-time, and overtime employment and this experience has led me to hold some strong views about the rigid standard forty-hour workweek and the opportunities to employees, employers, and society, of what is now considered "part-time" work.

I'm thirty-two years old and have been working half my years. I started at sixteen, working part-time as a car-hop for 35¢ an hour. To earn money for college, I added a part-time job as a nurse's aide (83¢ per hour) during high school. In the summers, I worked both jobs, averaging about sixty hours per week.

During college I worked part-time (50¢ an hour) on campus to pay part of my tuition. In the summers, I worked fifty hours a week at my hometown newspaper. After a year working forty hours a week as my college's news director after graduation, I worked about forty-eight hours a week for a radio-television news department; starting salary: $4,900 per annum. After two and a half years, I was forced to leave that job to have a child. No maternity leaves were then granted. My husband was working on his Master's degree and working part-time as a census taker, pizza maker, and substitute teacher. I then became a high school teacher—it wasn't right up my alley but the hours allowed me to have part of every day with my child. My husband had another part.

When we moved to Madison, I had resigned myself to being a nighttime and weekend waitress while my husband worked full-time days—to avoid child-care costs. In 1971, I was offered a half-time job at Extension. It seemed ideal. A year later, my husband also started working part-time. We struggled to get by on two part-time salaries but we figured that sharing the care of our child, the housework, and leisure was worth it. It was.

My job responsibilities expanded after a couple of years. I was asked to work full-time. We compromised on three-quarter time: thirty hours a week. The pay was less than three-quarters of a "full-time worker's" salary, but it was enough. A year later I was again asked to work forty hours a week and was offered a salary incentive and permission for a three-month leave of absence so the three of us could have a jaunt in Europe. I agreed, since it seemed I would not be considered or paid as a serious worker until I did. I was also trying to go to school part-time to earn a Master's degree as part of my job requirements. The combination of full-time work with part-time schooling was too much. My spirits suffered, and so did my family, from lack of my time for rest, family, leisure, or personal activities during that year, although I finally became accepted as a colleague. I demanded to go back to three-quarter time, promising the same productivity as I'd maintained on forty hours a week, plus the flexibility to appear at meetings, travel, and so on when necessary.

I've kept my promise. I come to work at 8:30 A.M. daily and leave at 2:30 P.M., eating lunch at my desk. When I'm at work, I work. I waste little time in kaffeeklatsches and chit-chat, although I do engage in work-oriented conversations and maintain good relationships with my coworkers. I arrange personal matters, doctor and dentist appointments, and so on on my own time, since I'm home two business hours of every day. I work mornings; my husband works afternoons. If our child is sick or on vacation from school, it presents no problem. Since I'm at work every day, my part-time status presents no inconvenience to other staff members. I have a thinking job and with ten hours a week to myself, I can think much more clearly and logically. Work becomes easier and less frantic. Studies have shown that an individual in most present-day work situations is only productive about six hours of any day. I certainly find it true for me. The quality of my work has improved considerably with the extra personal time for thought, rest, and energy renewal each day. The quantity of my work has not increased very much, nor has it decreased. I find the thirty-hour work week ideal (now that I actually earn three-quarters of a full-time salary) to enjoy my home, garden, social, family, and civic and personal interests. I'm trying to finish my thesis right now; when it's finished, I intend to rejoin the civic chorus, become more active in the neighborhood association and politics, read more, do some macrame and get more exercise, take a chair-caning class, spend much more time in the garden—and so on. My husband, who finished his schooling six years ago, has time for reading, writing poetry and plays, trying to construct a telescope, conversation, playing with his little boy, learning about photography, and so on.

We have lots to do every day, both of us. There are beds to make, two family meals and one school lunch to prepare, dishes to wash, lawn to mow, laundry, cleaning, grocery shopping, canoeing, bicycle riding, walking in the woods, and so on. We still don't have enough time to do *everything* we want to do, but we're grateful that we have more than most. Both of us working part-time is an ideal life-style that allows each of us a full share in the responsibilities, burdens, joys, excitements, and monotonies of both work and home worlds. It's a life-style benefiting both employers and employees. Further, I think the society benefits. There's no unfair burdening of one partner with full responsibility for bringing home the bacon and the other for cooking it. There is no economic dependency of one partner upon the other—but there is economic interdependency. Like the pioneers and cottage industrialists of our country's early days, but without their hardships, our work lives and home lives mesh. Our child benefits from full relationships with both his mother and his father, with neither of us bearing the total physical and psychological burdens of being his primary caretaker nor missing the joys of parenthood. We have been able to break out of the sex-role stereotypes imposed on both men and women only because we've had the time to share roles. My husband is unlikely to suffer an early heart attack or other health problems from the hassles and responsibilities of being his family's sole support or from all eyes looking to him to achieve, achieve, achieve. I can take care of myself if widowed. He's able to enjoy the pains and pleasures of family and domestic life of which most men are unaware. I'm not limited to a strict and frustrating domestic role that makes no use of my talents or training and can become stifling when it never comes in contact with a world outside of diapers and cookstoves. Nor am I burdened with the much over-glorified "dual role" of working full-time both inside and outside the home. Too many women spend eight hours a day at their jobs only to come home exhausted to full-time child care, housework, laundry, and cooking responsibilities.

My husband and I work part-time because we want to enjoy our son's development [but] the main reason, I think, is to find time to enjoy our *own* development . . . to enjoy more time that is our own. If we both retired right now we'd be quite happy and have plenty of interesting things to do and still never enough time to do them. We work because we must to be able to enjoy the little leisure we can eke out. Having a child, of course, means that we *must* dedicate more time to home responsibilities. I don't mind working . . . I'd rather work less but I can't live on less and still enjoy leisure the way I want to. (Testimony of Sheila Hogan Mulcahy to Wisconsin State Legislature Committee on Part-time and Flexible Time Employment, September 23, 1976.)

While Sheila Mulcahy may well represent only a minority of individuals who feel so strongly about the benefits of part-time work, she is by no means alone. For example, in a 1968 survey of women, it was estimated that ten million unemployed housewives age eighteen to forty-nine would supplement their roles at home with outside employment if part-time employment were available (Schonberger, 1970). Another survey of 3,500 people holding doctorates found that 11 percent of women holding doctorates and 8 percent of men, who were currently working full time, would prefer part-time work if they could get it (Eyde, 1975).

In the San Francisco area a contract funded by CETA for exploring the possibility of creating shared jobs for unemployed and low-income people found 268 applicants in four months. Of those, 80 percent were women, mostly between thirty-five and forty-four years old, and 20 percent were men between twenty-two and thirty-four. In addition, 72 percent of the people who wanted to share jobs have college degrees, and 15 percent were single parents. Forty-four percent were women heads of households, 22 percent were older workers, 22 percent were former employees who wanted to reenter the job market, 6 percent were minority in origin, 7 percent were students, and 13 percent of the applicants were currently working full time (Cunningham, 1976).

In addition to those who are of prime working age and interested in part-time work, there are millions of retired people who would gladly do some part-time work if they could find it and if it did not too seriously cut into their Social Security payments. The attention given in recent months to raising the mandatory retirement age from sixty-five to seventy results at least in part from the many people who are not ready to retire at sixty-five but who very well might be willing to continue on in a part-time capacity if such arrangements were possible. In the future, with increasing percentages of people fifty-five and above, they are likely to become a pressure group pushing not only for the possibility of later retirement but also for the possibility of tapering off from full-time to decreasing amounts of part-time. This could hardly fail to have important psychological benefits to those aging people who take part of their meaning in life from work identity.

Thus it is clear that there is a substantial minority currently employed and a very large number of people currently not working who would be interested in permanent part-time work were it available.

ADVANTAGES TO SOCIETY

In addition to the benefits to society from having women, the elderly, the handicapped, and others who do not wish to work full time able to find opportunities that meet their interests, there should be important social benefits in terms of reduced welfare costs and reduced costs of unemployment compensation. The Control Data Bindery in St. Paul has found that their part-time operation serves as a convenient entry point for those who would not otherwise be able to work, and over one hundred of their former employees now are working full time elsewhere rather than receiving welfare. The opportunity to find meaningful employment for those who have not worked before, or could not otherwise work, allows them to experience and understand the world of work and become productive contributors to society.

There are also advantages to society in creating the option of part-time work for those currently working full time, insofar as this would create new job openings for those who are unemployed and seeking work. At the same time, however, it must be said that the availability of part-time work might also bring many more people into the labor market, and could have an adverse effect on unemployment rates, even though it would lead to more jobs in total. This has been occurring in the economy even without new part-time jobs, as increasing percentages of women have chosen to work, so that despite record employment, there is also high unemployment.

DISADVANTAGES TO ORGANIZATIONS

Most disadvantages to the organization from part-time work are not likely to apply to well-designed permanent part-time or job-sharing programs. Scheduling will undoubtedly be more complex as part-time employment is scheduled to fit work hours preferred by individuals. For some part-time workers there is higher turnover because of lower commitment to the organization. This does not seem to have been the case with permanent part-time or job-sharing programs designed particularly to fit the needs of a segment of the population that is more mature and stable.

One problem can be additional costs for administration and especially for training of part-time employees. Insofar as it takes two or more employees to make the equivalent of one full-time employee, training costs are likely to be higher unless the training can be done in large batches. Similarly, if part-time employees are less capable than full-time employees, there may be a lessening in the quality of service or in productivity.

Another potential problem with permanent part-time and job sharing is that there may be a lack of continuity in the work flow and tasks will have to be completed by someone other than the person who starts them. This depends, of course, upon the nature of the technology being utilized by part-time employees. Many jobs are discrete and independent, with short time cycles, so that the issue would not arise, while others have longer time cycles and are heavily interdependent with other jobs or people.

In some organizations in which part-time employees are not permanent, they have lacked competence and dependability (poor attendance) and/or dressed sloppily. All these shortcomings are less likely to appear with PPT or job sharers, and with people who are doing highly skilled jobs.

In those organizations where part-time employees are not given proportionate fringe benefits they often have lower morale because of the extra pay deficiency beyond that for reduced hours. This morale problem apparently does not arise when benefits are prorated.

Another potential disadvantage can occur when the organization does not have full-time work available for employees on part-time who desire to change, and trained, qualified people leave for other organizations. For some organizations this could be costly; nevertheless, the Control Data Corporation is very proud about the number of people who have left the bindery to take full-time jobs, since many of the people who first worked at the bindery had not worked before or would have been unable to join any organization had it not been for the part-time opportunities. Thus the corporation sees the loss of employees as a contribution to society. And in that organization many of the employees do stay on to become full-time supervisors when their life conditions allow it.

In short, most of the disadvantages to organizations come about from treating part-timers as casual or intermittent help rather than seeing them as valuable employees, giving them proper training and responsibility and treating them accordingly.

DISADVANTAGES TO INDIVIDUALS

For the individual there are some important disadvantages to PPT work or job-sharing. Despite the good intentions of many organizations there can be little doubt that part-time employees are likely to advance more slowly than full-time employees during the same period, if at all. Until organizations become very serious about the whole concept of providing work arrangements for people at different life stages, with no penalty whatsoever, it is probable that the careers of those who work part-time will progress more slowly than the careers of full-time people, though part-timers may do better than they would have if they hadn't worked at all.

Another possible disadvantage is the reverse of the point made by the school superintendent who was so pleased that half-time pay often resulted in two-thirds time work. From the individual's point of view, part-time jobs, especially those that have professional or managerial responsibilities, may merely mean pay reduced more than actual work hours. Even Carol Greenwald (1973), a strong proponent of part-time work and a role model for thoughtful professionals, acknowledges some of the disadvantages of this kind of work: "The things one gives up by working part-time are some of those that make working enjoyable. One rarely takes a coffee break or has time to make friends during work hours. And, of course, I take a lot of work home, which I also did when I worked full time. I do not mind doing bank work in the evening. I just want some free hours with my daughter when she's awake." Many jobs, of course, require no more time investment than the scheduled time, and for those people in those kinds of part-time jobs, this disadvantage probably disappears.

There is an associated one, however, having to do with commuting. A person working part-time is likely to have commuting expenses that are proportionately higher as a percentage of wages than those of the person who works full-time. This is most true when the part-timer works on a daily basis and has to travel some distance to get to work. Those who work full days for part of the week, or work alternate weeks, suffer somewhat less in proportion to wages. Also, it may be harder working odd hours to make bus or train connections. But in the long run, the greater the number of people who work at nonstandard hours, the more that transportation systems can spread out their loads and the easier the commuting is likely to be. Until a greater proportion of the society changes, however, bus service and so on may not be as good at the odd hours. On the other hand, the person who works part-time and therefore does not have to travel during rush hours may find commuting less troublesome and possibly less expensive due to not having to sit in traffic jams, wasting time and gasoline.

These individual disadvantages are only relative; compared to not working at all and the burden of working full time, they are minor.

DISADVANTAGES TO SOCIETY

It is hard to see large disadvantages for society. If some people choose to work only part-time who could have productively worked full time, then there may be some overall loss in societal productive capacity, though it is hard to measure this against the presumed increase in peace of mind and attention to the family. This loss, however, depends on the nonwork interests that cause individuals to choose to work only part-time. If, for example, a particularly brilliant physicist were to work part-time and thereby decrease his or her actual problem solving efforts, it could be attributed as a loss to society. But if when not working the physicist engaged in nothing but regenerative activities, it might be that his or her creativity would ultimately be higher and stretch out over more productive years.

Another possible cost to society might arise if those working part-time become eligible for and later collect unemployment benefits that would not have been available otherwise. The net cost from such eventualities is likely to be quite low since alternative support would probably offset any savings from elimination of such benefits.

There are possible excess energy costs to society if part-time jobs and job sharing bring more people into the labor force who commute relatively frequently for the number of hours they actually work. The organizations that wish to remain open longer and are utilizing PPT work will consume more energy resources for light and heat. Again, these total costs are likely to be fairly small.

PEOPLE FOR WHOM THIS METHOD IS APPLICABLE

This has already been covered earlier in the chapter, but a quick review would be in order. A great deal of part-time work in the United States is done by women, and it is particularly helpful to women who would otherwise be forced to drop out in order to have and raise children. With women's participation in the work force rising, and with women's aspirations rising accordingly, PPT and job sharing provide them with excellent opportunities to not fall too far behind while giving sufficient attention and commitment to the family. Though some women will prefer not to have children or to continue full-time work within a few months of delivery, most will probably continue to prefer less than full-time work until children are in school.

The availability of part-time work can allow for more reasonable trade-offs between work and family. The experience of Katherine Darrow, a lawyer for the *New York Times*, demonstrates the possibilities. She

> . . . got the *Times* to agree to a three-day week in 1973 so she could spend more time with her two children.
>
> She found that she couldn't get her work done in three days so she switched to a four-day week. That was "perfect," she says. But the longer she stayed at the *Times*, the more responsibilities she acquired. She found that not only was she taking work home at night but that she was coming in to the office on the fifth day. Finally last year she quit pretending she was a part-timer and went back to a five-day week. Her children are now six and eight. (Main, 1977)*

---

* Excerpted from "Good Jobs Go Part Time" by Jeremy Main, *Money Magazine,* October 1977, by special permission; © 1977, Time Inc. All rights reserved.

It is also an excellent method for those who are near retirement and want to taper off, or who have retired but still have the energy and interest to continue working. At the other end of the age spectrum, PPT work is especially useful for allowing young people a chance to try out an organizational work life, and to get acquainted with the particular organization they work for.

The handicapped are another large group that would benefit from more availability of part-time and job-sharing. Many handicapped people do not have the physical energy to be able to work full time, but do not wish to be discards to society because of this.

Another group interested in PPT and job-sharing are those who have reached a plateau in an organization, yet do not need as much income as full-time work provides and would prefer to do at least some work so as not to feel useless. Many of those people might find that they could work with more vigor and be more effective if they did not have to work full time.

Similarly, there are an increasing number of people for whom full-time work is just not attractive. They are likely to include an increasing number of college graduates, for whom there will be fewer full-time meaningful jobs available because of increased numbers of graduates relative to jobs actually requiring college training. There are growing numbers of young men and women who are happy to work part-time in order to earn enough on which to "get by," but who would really rather not work full time at jobs that are less than fully satisfying.

All in all, there are many people who at some stage during their career would like and benefit from the opportunity for permanent part-time or job-sharing. Organizations that recognize this and create opportunities for occasional periods of reduced work hours are likely to find new sources of talent and a lower turnover rate of valuable employees.

6
CHOOSING APPROPRIATE TIME ARRANGEMENTS

In the preceding chapters we have looked at the recently developed methods for scheduling time and examined the varying needs of people at different stages of their lives. So far we have linked life-cycle and demographic data to preferred schedule choices for individuals, and have suggested some of the organizational problems that various schedules help to solve. But actual choice of schedules is a complicated process. Schedulers, material planners, capacity analysts, and others are likely to be affected by such choices and ought to be involved in such changes.

We will now turn to a framework we have developed that can be used by managers to analyze their organizations' needs and possibilities in order to make good decisions about work schedules. In this chapter we will show how to match the cyclical time *demands* for work with *people* and with *schedules* in a way that leads to better coverage of work needs, greater commitment of employees, better utilization of human resources, and, in many instances, greater productivity. For convenience, we call this the DIPS method of scheduling (*D*emand *P*eople *S*chedules), which connotes cyclical fluctuations.

We will then give examples from companies using this kind of de-mand/people/schedules reasoning to achieve positive results.

The kind of reasoning we will describe is best applied on a unit-by-unit basis within the organization, paying attention to the work within the unit as well as its interrelationships with other units. Each unit is likely to have its own particular mix of work demands, people, and schedules, and the design of the mix is most successful when the unit's particular needs are taken into account. The same kind of reasoning is appropriate for the entire organization where there is great homogeneity across subunits. What is important is the reasoning and analysis.

MODEL FOR CHOOSING APPROPRIATE TIME ARRANGEMENTS FOR ORGANIZATIONAL SUBUNITS

First we will outline the model and then deal with each point in it specifically.

1. Analyze the nature of the unit's work in terms of the demands for output and coverage that come from the unit's environment and technology: What are the sources of the demands, when is more/less output needed, when are people needed to do what, and what are the predictable variations in demand for work?

2. Determine a schedule that would provide coverage to fit the needs analyzed in (1).

3. Analyze the existing work force to see what kinds of time arrangements are *likely* to be attractive to it. This should result in a segmented analysis for different people in the unit. Where are employees in the life cycle? What are their needs for money, for time away from work, for challenging and meaningful work?

4. Assess the fit between the provisional schedule determined in (2) and the likely interests of people who already work there.

5. If the provisional schedule meets both the needs of the people who already work there and the demands for work, choose that schedule.

6. If it does not fit, then

    a) examine whether it is possible to affect the timing and nature of demand to fit employee preferences. If not possible,

    b) assess what kinds of people would like to work the hours needed and whether they are available within the community. Then,

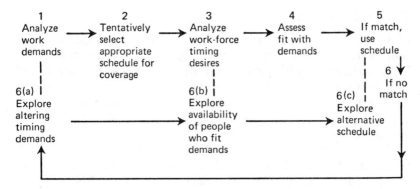

Fig. 6.1 DIPS model for choosing appropriate time arrangements.

c) look for an alternative schedule which can meet the needs of those who are (and could be) available to work as well as meeting existing or altered demand.

WORK DEMANDS

We will look first at the nature of the work itself—the way in which the environment of a unit and its technology create "demands" for output and coverage. The first thing to look at is the flow of work within each unit. Very few units in any organization have a steady demand pace at all times. The demand for output and rapid pace can vary hourly, daily, weekly, monthly, seasonally, yearly, or in several-year cycles. Demand varies with (a) the output of other units, as when there must be reports completed in order for other units to do their work; (b) required inputs to other units, as when the EDP department must have data from a unit by a certain time in order to produce regular analyses; (c) fluctuations in consumer habits, as when customers bunch up at certain hours, on certain days, or in certain seasons; (d) economic cycles, as when sales soar during full employment and sag when there is slack in the economy; (e) the weather, as with recreational business; and (f) natural cycles in the production technology, as when batches of steel or other products have long "incubation," or set-ups are periodically needed.

Demand Smoothing

Many of these variations are not within the control of the particular unit receiving the demands, although organizations often try to invent ways to smooth out the peaks and valleys of demand for output, and thus for the presence of employees. For many parts of organizations, *inventory* is used to smooth demands. But for some parts, and for many organizations without physical products that can be inventoried, other methods are sought.

Such organizations can often "fake inventory"—think through the nature of the rules that created the uneven demand and alter those to spread it out more evenly. For example, the state of New Hampshire, among others, eliminated long waiting lines the week before April 15th, when license plates had to be picked up, by changing the dates for obtaining new license plates to coincide with driver's birthdays. A similar procedure was adopted for obtaining drivers' licenses. Thus the demand was spread out over the entire year rather then being allowed to bunch up in one month.

Another variation is to allow demand to accumulate, creating a backlog and allowing orders or people to wait before the product or service is delivered. Thus, "queues" are a way of managing demand. Other organizations have tried to alter demand by limiting hours of customer service—refusing to respond to demand except within certain time periods—or by eliminating particular products that place unusually difficult stresses on the organization. Subcontracting is an analogous way of "exporting" the demand, reducing its effects on the unit and altering the need for employee presence.

Organizations with highly cyclical business often look to acquire or develop other products that have complementary cycles with opposite peaks and valleys. A classic case would be the air-conditioning equipment manufacturer who seeks ways to produce heating equipment. This method is difficult to successfully implement, but very helpful when possible.

Pricing, promotions, and rationing are all ways of trying to alter the timing of demand. The phone company is an equipment-intensive operation. To try to spread demand so that it needs less equipment for peak periods, it charges less for off-hours calls and advertises the bargain to lure at least some callers into avoiding business hours when demand is highest. The phone company also adjusts its hiring on a daily basis to fit demand, laying off employees not needed. Since it hires young single women who are usually not the sole sources of support for their families and who value time off, the company can vary the work force without creating dissatisfaction.

Finally, it is important to know that even where demand smoothing is not possible for an entire unit, it is often possible for subunits or portions of the work. A unit with great demand fluctuations may be able, for example, to produce parts that are not assembled, or work steadily at portions of the unit's activities even while varying others.

In terms of thinking about appropriate work schedules, it probably is easiest to first take the existing demands as given. Where there is high variation, however, it is useful to ask whether the demand really is fixed or whether it can be altered by some of the devices mentioned above.*

Demands from Technology

Another way of looking at work demands is in terms of the nature of the organization's technology or production process. Differing technologies call for differing responses from employees in terms of amounts of attention and care needed, skill required, and general commitment to the work. When technology is routine and mechan‐ ical, calling for little skill or attentiveness on the part of employees, then the question of coverage becomes one of having sufficient numbers of bodies present. When the technology demands generally high skills, individual skills that are not widely possessed, or great attention and commitment, then coverage problems become more complex because people cannot be easily substituted for one another. Furthermore, some technologies cannot function at all if there are people missing, while others can allow for a considerable amount of independent activity, even when various functions are not being fulfilled at any particular time.

The assembly line is, of course, the classic example of the totally interdependent operation in which someone must be at each station or the product being assembled will be deficient. Yet even assembly lines can often have some of their operations "decoupled" from others. Production planners have been inventive at creating opportunities for

---

* For a more detailed discussion of techniques for leveling demand, see Jay R. Galbraith's *Organization Design,* Chapter 15, "Organization and Environment: An Example of Production Smoothing."

"banking" of parts between some stations, or for using relief workers to enhance capacity of particular stations. Many other types of technologies require even less that every "station" be staffed at all times, because there is low interdependence among the activities of the unit and one person's work can proceed at a different pace and time from others in the unit.

Finally, as implied above, the interdependencies of the unit with other units or with its environment also affect the flow of work. Just as within units some individuals can work effectively without regard to whether or not others are present, so too within organizations some units can work relatively independently of other units. Nevertheless, some units require either frequent interfacing with other units, or periodic, time-bounded interfacing in which one unit's input becomes the other's output, and vice versa. Of course, interunit interdependencies may also be examined for partial decoupling.

In general, *the greater a unit's interdependencies with other units, the more difficult it will be to allow flexibility in a new schedule. However, the greater the peaks and valleys of work demands, the greater the opportunity and benefits from devising an altered schedule. And the greater the variation in work demands, the greater the likelihood that atypical members of the working population will have to be found to work the requisite hours in order to meet the demands.*

NATURE OF THE PEOPLE AT WORK

The next step in choosing the appropriate mix for an organization is to look at the interests and desires of the present work force. Without expensive or elaborate surveys, it is possible to use rough demographic data to make some estimates of when core employees are likely to want to work, how hard they would like to work, and how central work is to their lives.* These matters can be determined by looking at the age of the work force, its sexual composition, its marital status, and the number and ages of children. A large, urban insurance company employing thousands of single females between the ages of eighteen and twenty-four, as does John Hancock, can expect quite differ-

---

* It is, of course, possible to determine employee interests directly, through questionnaires or interviews, though the danger in asking is that expectations are likely to be raised. Nevertheless, an employer who is committed to such changes might as well ask.

ent responses to work and working hours than does a small-town, small-size insurance company like United Life, where the work force consists mostly of relatively immobile married people from twenty-five to forty-five, who have children and families and are likely to want a career.

If the company's demands do not fit the characteristics of the existing work force, and the demands cannot be altered to fit, then the next question to be addressed is what kinds of employees are available, not only within the community, or in terms of skills, but also in terms of their likely desired hours of work. It should be noted that employee willingness to work odd hours, or overtime, or reduced hours, will vary with the rate of unemployment; nevertheless, while some people temporarily might be willing to work at inconvenient times due to necessity, the general willingness to work nonstandard hours is a function of employee place in the life cycle. If the organization has work-flow demands that are not easily fit into standard work hours, then it can make useful predictions about availability of employees based on the demographic makeup of the community.

An organization may also discover new sources of employees to work odd hours if it is determined that the odd hours can be grouped in such a way that they form part-time jobs or overlapping shifts. For example, the "mother's hours" of 9:30 to 2:30 utilized by Massachusetts Mutual, tap a previously unavailable segment of the work force. Similarly, college students and others in the eighteen to twenty-four age range are often willing to work unusual hours in return for blocks of time off for education or leisure. And those near or in retirement may prefer varying hours if they are not too taxing.

SCHEDULES

After the nature of work demands has been examined along with availability of employees who are likely to be interested in working at times to meet those demands, then a work schedule that will meet the needs of each unit can be selected from the infinite scheduling possibilities. The guidelines offered in earlier chapters for relating which scheduling methods are suitable to which population can be used to select a schedule or schedules within which there will be sufficient numbers of employees to cover the work—and to cover it well, because their work times fit optimally with their other life needs.

By now it should be clear that we believe that employees who are allowed to work at times that mesh with where they are in their lives are certainly likely to be more satisfied, more committed to the organization and to the accomplishment of organizational ends. While there is ample evidence to suggest that satisfaction is not necessarily correlated with productivity, we believe that, all other things being equal, the employee who works at times that are best for him or her is also likely to be more productive.

GUIDELINES FOR SCHEDULE SELECTION

To help in the schedule selection process, we have developed a series of propositions or guidelines. These rough rules of thumb are intended to be useful in focusing attention on likely schedules for particular populations, but are not presumed to be definitive or limiting. They can serve as indicators for further investigation.

1. The greater the number of schedule choices employees have, the greater their satisfaction. Wherever possible, offer options.

2. The greater the peaks and valleys of work demands, the greater the likelihood of benefits from alternative schedules.

3. Similarly, the greater the amount of overtime currently being utilized, the greater the likelihood of benefits from alternative schedules.

4. The greater the need to extend service hours, the greater the need for altered schedules; flexible working hours is the least difficult way to accomplish this if there is a heterogeneous work force, because of natural dispersion of hours. Permanent part-time and compressed weeks can also accomplish lengthening of hours.

5. The greater the availability of unmarried individuals, students, couples with no children, couples with grown children, and employees without a working spouse, the greater the likelihood of finding employees willing and satisfied to work at nonstandard times.

6. The greater the difficulty of finding employees to work at the right times, or with the requisite skills, the greater the need for utilizing permanent part-time, flexible working hours, or compressed weeks, in that order, to locate desired employees.

7. The greater the number of employees who are working mothers, the greater the attractiveness of flexible working hours and (to a lesser extent), permanent part-time, and the less the attractiveness of compressed weeks.

8. Where regular, around-the-clock operations are required, compressed week schedules are likely to be most attractive to employees.

9. The greater the number of (a) people over fifty-five, (b) mothers with small children, and (c) students, the greater the attractiveness to employees of less than full-time arrangements.

10. Where the technology is capital intensive or continuous process, compressed-week schedules are likely to be most appropriate, especially when combined with flexible working hours.

11. The less interdependence among jobs/employees/units, the greater the payoffs from flexible working hours.

12. The greater the creativity called for by jobs, the greater the payoffs from flexible working hours and from compressed weeks, with blocks of time off and fewer "startups."

13. The more physically/mentally/emotionally demanding the work, the lower the appropriateness of compressed-week schedules.

14. In urban areas, employees are likely to prefer flexible working hours because of the traffic and time savings; in rural areas, compressed weeks are likely to be preferred because of blocks of time off. Either of these preferences may be moderated by distance and preferred leisure activities.

EXAMPLES OF ORGANIZATIONS UTILIZING INNOVATIVE SCHEDULING

It should be instructive to look at several organizations and the ways in which they utilize the type of reasoning presented to adopt effective work schedules. An example of an organization with an extreme scheduling problem is Harrah's in Reno, Nevada. A resort hotel and gambling establishment, it is open twenty-four hours a day, 365 days a year. For years it had difficulty trying to get coverage using standard round-the-clock shift work. Several years ago, when alternative work schedules began to be popularized, the personnel department decided to offer self-designed schedules to employees to see if it could get better coverage. The department found that some employees preferred three long days and a short one, others preferred a four-day week, while still others preferred a standard five-day week. Once employees were allowed to choose the kind of work hours they preferred, the organization's scheduling difficulties disappeared. The people available for work in Reno include a high proportion of divorced women with children, young singles, and others who are willing to work odd hours in return for time off during periods when they desire it.

Similarly, airlines have developed an elaborate bidding system to allow pilots and flight attendants to select schedules that fit their personal needs and preferences. The airline says when it will need people and then allows employees, on the basis of a complicated formula involving seniority and maximum consecutive flying hours, to bid for desired schedules. Such scheduling systems require elaborate record-keeping procedures to ensure control and coverage, but are not quite as difficult or different from established procedures as they at first appear. They do require managers to think clearly about what coverage is actually needed, but that is not an unreasonable expectation for managers.

The Control Data Corporation has probably utilized life-cycle/schedule reasoning most extensively of all American companies. As mentioned in Chapter 5, the corporation's concern for social issues led them to design a plant in St. Paul, Minnesota, that could provide work opportunities for ghetto residents. The corporation particularly wanted to allow mothers needing supplemental income and female heads of households with dependent children the chance to work despite the lack of day-care facilities. It determined that part-time work would be viable and desired, then set out to find a product that could be produced by a part-time work force. It decided that the extensive manuals for computer operation needed by the company could be produced in that way, and that the skills needed would be available, and they opened a bindery in the ghetto in 1971. It collates, binds, and mails computer manuals and documents to Control Data's customers, and performs similar contracted services for outsiders.

The bindery runs from 6:00 A.M. to 10:00 P.M., with employees choosing from three shift options: three, four, or six hours. They can select the shifts to fit life needs, working early morning, midday, after school, or in the evening. The plant employs 40–50 percent female heads of households, 15 percent handicapped persons who cannot work full time, and about 35 percent students. Employees are paid the same hourly rate as full-time workers in comparable job classifications at other Control Data plants; benefits are prorated proportionate to hours worked.

Supervisors in the plant work standard eight-hour shifts; almost all of the supervisors started as part-time employees and expressed interest in full-time work as their life situations changed—children grew up, or a bedridden spouse or dependent parent died, for example.

As a result of these arrangements, which fit working hours to life style of available employees, the productivity per capita per hour at this plant is much higher than at other plants of the company. Annual volume is about $500,000 and operations were profitable enough to cause the company to build a new 15,000 square-foot facility in 1974. Employees are delighted at the opportunities afforded them and work with great dedication and commitment. They want to keep their jobs, want to do well, and can devote themselves to work when they are there because other life needs do not interfere. The company believes there is also less fatigue on the shorter shifts, and that there is less loss of productive effort compared to those who work longer shifts. Both company and employees benefit from the arrangements.

An organization that is in the process of altering its schedules to try to deal with severe turnover problems (50 percent yearly) and high absenteeism, especially on weekends, is the Laconia State School for the mentally retarded, in New Hampshire. As a residential institution for the handicapped, it must have seven-days-a-week, twenty-four-hour coverage. The three-shift schedule—6:30 A.M.–3:00 P.M.; 2:30 P.M.–11:00 P.M.; 10:45 P.M.–6:45 A.M.—has not functioned well for many reasons, including understaffing and low pay. We have worked with people in the scheduling office to help them go through a variation of the DIPS method for scheduling.

Careful analysis of the time demands in the residences resulted in the realization that heaviest coverage needs were 7:30 A.M.–12:30 P.M., 4:00 P.M.–8:00 P.M., and 4:00 A.M.–7:00 A.M. These periods include meals, medical appointments, waking up, and evening recreation. New schedules would have to provide for maximum coverage during these hours.

A set of optional schedules was devised using these three time periods as "core hours" for each of three shifts. Those on the day and evening shifts turned out to be interested in four-day weeks with longer daily hours; night-shift employees preferred eight-hour, five-day weeks. Each person on all the shifts was allowed to indicate preference for his/her starting times from among several half-hour intervals outside of core time. Once all employees were polled, the schedulers were able to assign everyone to his or her preferred shift and starting time, with days off at least in part falling on current days off. The new schedule includes four-day and five-day weeks with modified flexible hours.

Just by natural choice (related to life situations as we shall show), the entire week was covered with present employees, with only a few hours of exceptions. The holes in the schedule can easily be covered by new hires, who can be recruited to fill specific schedule openings.

As predicted, employees chose schedule options that fit their places in the life cycle. Those who chose day shift are the older employees who have grown children, older adults unmarried or childless, and some young marrieds without children. Those day-shift people with school-age children have chosen to start later than the former 6:30 A.M. starting time in order to accommodate to day-care center arrangements or to see children off on school buses.

The evening-shift workers tend to be very young singles, eighteen to twenty-five years old, who are night owls and enjoy partying or closing the bars after they get out of work. Some have chosen to start the shift an hour earlier so they can get off by 10 P.M. to start their nocturnal activities earlier. And the late-night shift workers tend to be family people where both parents are working and divide time home with children. The night-shift person arrives home to awaken the rest of the family and get them started; some have chosen slightly earlier starting times so they can return home earlier and get their families up.

Thus the new schedule options allow people to adjust working hours to family situations, give those who want it three consecutive days off (making weekend work less onerous), and provide better coverage at key times. Though the new schedules are just being implemented as of this writing, we are confident that turnover, absenteeism, and morale should all improve, resulting in better care of residents.

One unpredicted side benefit has already been realized. Scheduling overlapping coverage at core hours has resulted in greater availability of employees at times when they can be more productive. First- and second-shift employees are now available in the afternoon to teach basic living skills to the children when they are awake and most receptive. Thus while the shift is still understaffed overall, more care is available when it can be best utilized, leading to greater productivity.

A company with an entirely different kind of problem, and therefore a different type of employee population, is the Davis and Furber Machinery Company in North Andover, Massachusetts. A manufacturer of machinery that produces fiber, its business activities are closely tied to the fortunes of the carpet industry, which is highly cyclical depending on number of housing starts and other aspects of the overall economy. The business tends to be boom or bust in two-to-four-year cycles, necessitating frequent layoffs or the employment of more employees than are needed. That could lead to loss of skilled employees or disproportionate expenses. Nevertheless, the company has been able over the years to retain a large number of long-term employees by finding people willing to live their lives around extended layoff periods when business is slack. These employees tend to be older, with children who are teenagers or out of the house and wives who work to provide supplemental income. Rather than get other jobs when they are laid off for several months, they prefer to collect unemployment, plan long vacations, and prepare to work intensively and save money again when business picks up. The company prefers to have employees who are skilled remain with them, so that it is to the company's advantage to have people who are willing to accept long layoffs rather than work reduced number of hours during slack times or seek other employment. And the employees have self-selected themselves into those whose life-styles fit this seasonal pattern.

A company trying to overcome a different kind of problem, mentioned earlier, is United Life of Concord, New Hampshire. Several years ago, before it was widely adopted, the company initiated flexible working hours. Somewhat to the company's surprise, a very high proportion of employees preferred to come to work at the earliest possible working hour—7:30 A.M.—and were ready to leave at 3:30 P.M. This was different from many organizations on flexible working hours around the world, where employees naturally spread starting time before and after the previous fixed start. But United Life's work force, coming from a small town, is fairly homogeneous and mostly prefers an early start and finish in order to leave daylight hours for family and recreation. As a result there are coverage problems from 3:30 P.M. onward, creating difficulties especially for West Coast personnel who want information by phone in the afternoon. The company had been thinking of eliminating the flexible working hours arrangement; we have advised a unit-by-unit analysis of where coverage is needed and the possibility of employing some part-time people, possibly college students in their area, who could be trained to look up information and answer questions from 3:30 P.M. to 6:30 P.M. This would not only solve the coverage problem but also extend the service hours during which information could be obtained from outside.

Thus, the method of analysis suggested in this chapter can lead to the kind of inventive solutions that not only solve a particular work problem but may provide better service, better quality, or better productivity. When schedules, people, and demand are aligned, both human needs and organizational ends are better served.

Another organization uses demographics in quite a different way. McDonald's Corporation needs a lot of help at certain hours when there's a rush for food, and only skeletal coverage at other hours. The corporation has found that hiring young employees, from sixteen to twenty-two years old, allows them to staff for peak loads on a less than forty-hour-per-week basis, and also creates a young, fresh image for the organization.

A German department store, Eyrich in Tuttlingen, handles peak-load problems in a different way: department stores have different periods of the day in which there is a considerable amount of business and other periods in which things are very slow. This particular store had difficulty in trying to schedule people at the right time until it decided to go on a self-scheduling, mostly commission system. The store decided that the employees, predominantly women, would schedule at appropriate times while following their own self-interest if they were given the opportunity. This indeed proved to be the case. The women even arranged to provide for emergency coverage within ten minutes should the store get very busy at unexpected times. A further benefit to the store was that employees no longer were unwilling to help out in other departments when there were customers lined up, not only because it was in their own individual economic interest to help customers as much as possible, but also because they knew that by keeping customers satisfied and lines short they could keep the privileges of setting their own hours.

Yet another organization that has gone to differentiated staffing is United Parcel Service. In that organization the drivers need to be out all day to make delivery runs economical, while those inside who sort and handle packages do not need to be there full time during the

day and in fact are needed at odd hours to deal with incoming ship-
ments. The company decided to use part-time staffing inside, hiring
many college students to work half-day shifts. Since the college students usually leave the firm after graduation, the company has considerable flexibility in terms of staffing levels. This flexibility is possible
because the work is not highly technical and employees are inter-
changeable with minimal amounts of training. It should also be mentioned here that this differentiated system was at the heart of the long
recent strike against United Parcel Service, which originated with the
truck drivers. The drivers were in part concerned because they wanted
to be certain that should something happen to their ability to drive
trucks there might still be a possibility of working inside the company
at full hours. It should also be noted that the company pays its part-
time employees only 60–70 percent of the hourly wages that its full-
time truck drivers are paid, and that this differential is greater than the
one envisioned by the concept of permanent part-time work, where
wages and benefits per hour are assumed to be the same and it is only
number of hours per week that is reduced.

Once an organization begins to think in terms of DIPS scheduling, the possibilities for arrangement of working hours to fit with
employee needs are greatly expanded. For example, the *Wall Street
Journal* (Evans, 1976) reported on a number of companies, including
Weyerhauser, McDonald's, and United Air Lines, which are currently
allowing some executives to work at home when a high degree of concentration is necessary to complete a particular task or project.
Among the benefits cited were less commuting time, an informal
atmosphere without telephones interrupting, and the ability to see the
family and children more easily. While such a system is not likely to
spread rapidly and is probably appropriate mostly for executives, who
are not tied to a production technology, we can foresee a day when
technological developments will make it possible for many to work at
home at least some of the time. Recently, for example, LIFT, Inc.
hired eleven handicapped people, putting computer terminals in their
homes and allowing them to do programming work at home (*Wall
Street Journal*, August 30, 1977).

Another interesting hours variation has been put into practice by
Mt. Auburn Hospital in Cambridge, Massachusetts, as a response to
employee dissatisfaction with inequities in sick-leave practice: Some
employees had never used the accumulated allowable days of sick
leave, while others managed to "get sick" exactly the number of days

allotted each year. As a result, the hospital instituted a policy called "earned time," allowing employees to earn up to eight days per year of personal time and accrue up to seventy-two days which they are allowed to take without having to pretend that they are sick. This also allows employees who know about upcoming events that will necessitate taking personal time off to notify their supervisors in advance so that coverage, vital in a hospital, can be arranged for easily. Similarly, Harmon Kardon employees can earn "idle time" by completing work in less than eight hours; the time is used for educational classes, often taught by fellow workers.

One of the early pioneers in propagating flexible work hours, Willi Haller, has now begun to advocate the concept of the flexible year. He argues that maximum flexibility would be obtained in meeting individual needs if the individual and employer negotiated what a standard number of hours in a work year would be, and then employees could arrange to work from 10 percent to 90 percent of the standard work year with proportional pay and benefits. Haller argues that this would help to relieve unemployment and would also be particularly suitable for recent high school and college graduates who are entering the work force for the first time and might prefer not to work full time. Similarly, it would help those who are nearing retirement and might like to continue working at a reduced number of hours. He also mentions that those in their middle years periodically might like to take time to spend with young children (Haller, 1977).

CONCLUSION

The possibilities of variations in work schedule are limited only by the constraints of technology, the constraints of employees' interest based on their place in the life cycle, and the imagination of the schedule designers. There are few enough organizational innovations and practices that allow both the employer to better meet organizational needs and the employee to better make trade-offs between work and nonwork interests; the methods and concepts presented in this book can contribute both to organizational effectiveness and human happiness. And since all of these methods can be linked with organizational development tools, as explained in the next chapter, we believe that those who wish to change organizations would benefit from using an altered work arrangement/adult-life-cycle, DIPS methodology as part of their repertoire.

7
ALTERNATIVE WORK SCHEDULES
AND ORGANIZATION DEVELOPMENT

INTRODUCTION

The preceding chapters in this book demonstrate the potential benefits for organizations and individuals inherent in alternative work patterns and in the DIPS method of scheduling to take people's place in
the life cycle into account. On this basis alone, it is worth exploring
new scheduling arrangements. But we believe that there are further
potential benefits for organizations if the introduction and implementation of new schedules is done properly. Organization development
practitioners have not as yet appreciated the ways in which alternative
work patterns may be utilized to further OD goals, yielding an important "multiplier effect" for change efforts. This chapter shows how
this may be done.

ORGANIZATION DEVELOPMENT: KEY ELEMENTS

Although organization development (OD) is a difficult concept to
capture in a few sentences, there seems to be agreement that at its
roots is the intent to make organizations both more humane and more
effective through planned change. Beckhard (1969) defines organization development as "an effort (1) *planned* (2) *organization-wide,* and
(3) *managed* from the top, to (4) increase *organization effectiveness*

and *health* through (5) planned interventions in the organization's 'processes,' using behavioral-science knowledge.'' OD work builds on trust, openness, independence, shared influence, choice, and the response to felt needs. This chapter will link these concepts to alternative work schedules.

In its early history, OD was largely confined to interventions that attempted to alter attitudes and improve interpersonal relations at the top of an organization. As a consequence, OD was, and still most often is, a trickle-down strategy intended to gradually envelop lower-level managers and eventually the hourly workers at the bottom of the hierarchy. Attention was paid primarily to interpersonal, group, and organizational processes; it was assumed that fundamental structural changes would more or less naturally emerge from these improved relationships as needed, thereby improving effectiveness and reinforcing new attitudes and behavior. In this way the organization could constantly renew itself.

Because new structures could be and often were subverted by those with hostile attitudes, OD practitioners concentrated on the attitudes and relationships, somehow giving less weight to the equally difficult problem of attitudinal fadeout without structures supporting the new attitudes. And since attitudes throughout an organization often reflect those at the top, and changes below need top management support, OD practitioners aimed their efforts high.

Only recently have horizons broadened to include structural interventions as a starting point from which attitudes can be induced, leading to further changes in the desired directions. Structural interventions have begun to occur at any place or level in an organization and include blue- and white-collar hourly workers in addition to managers (Hackman, 1977a, Cummings and Molloy, 1977, etc.). Issues of both humaneness and effectiveness can be addressed even at the lowest levels of organizations. Management By Objectives (MBO), autonomous work groups, Scanlon plans, job enrichment, and job enlargement are increasingly being used by OD practitioners as parts of more comprehensive programs of planned change.

Although *time* is a structural variable with a great deal of impact on behavior, its significance as the basis for OD interventions has not been widely appreciated. Alternative schedules have often been adopted without awareness of how they may contribute to OD efforts. Even skilled OD practitioners have supported new schedules without seeing important possible linkages to other OD efforts and objectives

(Golembiewski et al., 1974). It is our position that some work schedules, as a function of time, have considerable potential for OD activity. It is therefore the purpose of this chapter to explore the implications for OD of the various work schedules covered in this book.

OD PAYOFFS

For the OD practitioner, the introduction of alternative work schedules provides a number of opportunities to:

1. Positively affect large numbers of employees

2. Demonstrate that taking into account more of the whole person—at work and away from it—will improve both performance and satisfaction

3. Improve such tangible performance indicators as absenteeism, turnover, tardiness

4. Enhance employee ability to make *choices* consistent with current life-style needs (at least in organizations where more than one schedule is available to choose from), or to choose work hours on a daily or weekly basis

5. Improve morale, which is both worthwhile in itself and useful for gaining goodwill toward further OD efforts

6. Gain personal or departmental credibility as to knowledge and competence.

These are not inconsiderable advantages. There are few methods that are likely to have such widespread benefits yet be so readily implementable. And many other OD activities are likely to be made more acceptable by a successful implementation of an appropriate mix of altered schedules.

Choice

It is important to note that one of the key issues in relation to altered schedules is the need for creating an array of schedule choices from which employees can choose. Although the methods described in Chapter 6 for selecting a schedule may lead to the same schedule for everyone in a few small companies with restricted demand characteristics and a homogeneous work force, most organizations will have a wider range of needs and work-force characteristics. Any mix of altered work arrangements that allows employees some *choice* over their own work times will reinforce OD values of independence and autonomy.

Furthermore, though for convenience we have talked about people at different stages of the life cycle as if stages were fixed, the whole thrust of the analysis is that people's needs in regard to work schedules change over time. The employee who is happy to work part-time today will leave unless he or she can work full time at a later stage, and may want part-time again at other life points. Organizations that allow employees to choose among scheduling arrangements (provided that the total arrangements meet the demands of the organization) will build employee commitment not only to present jobs, but also to the organization over a longer term. Thus people who are valuable resources will be less likely to leave, or to work half-heartedly in response to fixed schedules that do not fit life needs.

While many benefits can accrue to organizations using any one of the schedules described in this book, the OD practitioner needs to be especially concerned with the maximization of individual choice.

Once established, any fixed schedule gives individuals no further control over the allocation of their time between work and nonwork activities. If individuals enjoy the fixed arrangement, it is valued as a benefit, such as is Blue Cross, life insurance, good pay, and pleasant surroundings. It makes life satisfying and work more attractive, but does not lead to growth on the job.

By contrast, choice among schedules vests in individuals responsibility for an appropriate distribution of time between their needs and those of the organization. Whereas fixed schedules stress dependence, chosen, alterable schedules stress independence. The former is the characteristic of an immature person, the latter of a responsible adult. In Herzberg's (1966) terms,* fixed schedules would be "satisfiers" and flexible schedules "motivators."

_____

* "Satisfiers," sometimes called "hygiene factors," make a job appealing or unappealing but do not induce effort toward improved performance. They include environment, benefits, wages, and supervision. "Motivators" induce effort toward improved performance. They include autonomy, variety, challenge, and promotional opportunities.

The issue that distinguishes chosen from fixed schedules is control. Herzberg proposes that self-control or "autonomy" is valued by individuals, and acts as a continuing incentive to perform well. This thesis is consistent with a considerable body of theory and empirical evidence including Herzberg's own research.

Argyris identifies autonomy as a factor in achieving psychological success; McGregor has expressed its importance in his Theory Y; Rollo May relates the absence of it to feelings of powerlessness and indiscriminate violence; Erik Erikson includes it as a characteristic of a mature adult in his eight stages of man. A multitude of surveys also show that workers strongly desire freedom from tight controls, a wish confirmed by our own research. Time after time we have been told by workers that one of the things they most like about flexible working hours is the self-respect they feel from being treated as responsible people.* Choice among work schedules or within a schedule enhances self-esteem.

Rearranged Schedules as a Trust Builder

Usually starting at the top, and addressing attitudes first, OD programs attempt to develop enough trust so that open, honest exchange can take place. This exchange produces the "valid information" to which Argyris (1970) refers as the basis for identifying problems to which the organization will devote itself. Structures then are expected to emerge that increase organizational effectiveness, reinforce newly developed attitudes and behavior, and promote individual learning. Approached this way, the diffusion process is invariably a long one, often taking years, if ever, to have a substantial impact on hourly workers (Blake and Mouton, 1964).

A contribution to the time-consuming character of many comprehensive OD programs is the slow process by which trust is built. Trust requires experience to confirm it. Otherwise, there is risk in relying on others before one knows they are trustworthy. Frequent recourse to old forms of behavior with which one is familiar, in spite of OD efforts to cultivate alternatives, is hardly surprising until there is sufficient experience to confirm the reliability of the alternatives.

---

*   Rosabeth Kanter reports that her research suggests that "dignity" is a motivator of exceptional power.

The question, then, is how to utilize the introduction of altered work arrangements to provide *choice* and build *trust*. If this can be done, then gains from the schedules chosen will have payoffs above and beyond those directly related to the particular methods. As a result, other OD efforts may be encouraged, supported, or initiated. We believe in organizational development as a field, and support its general spread and utilization. Although all schedules we discuss can be integrated into an OD program, we have been most enthusiastic about the potential of flexible working hours for furthering OD objectives. That is the method that allows the most choice and encourages the most trust on a day-to-day basis. If an employee can choose work schedules at a firm every few years to fit life stages, that is an enormous expansion of choice. But the right to choose working hours daily, to fit variations with the life stage, is an even greater creation of the opportunity for employee choices, and often induces supervisory trust.

Since a system of flexible working hours not only has inherent in it the most important payoffs for subsequent OD efforts but also the potential for being combined with all the other methods in the book, we shall discuss in detail how it may be introduced in a way that maximizes OD payoffs. However, the same general procedures also apply to introduction of other alternative work schedules—and indeed to the introduction of structural interventions such as job enrichment, job enlargement, and autonomous work groups. For example, data cited in Chapter 2 about the resistance to job enrichment by older, long-term employees (Van Maanen and Schein, 1971) suggest that utilizing life-cycle analysis and the implementation methods described below would be useful for changes other than rearranged work schedules.

FLEXIBLE WORKING HOURS— BUILDING FURTHER OD EFFORTS

Trust Inducement

Because most flexible working hours systems allow employees to work before and/or after supervisors are present, flexible hours give supervisors valuable experience in trusting subordinates. Thus flexible scheduling is primarily a *trust-inducing* strategy for change rather than one that is *trust based*. Enough trust by supervisors is needed for them to be willing to adopt flexible schedules, but thereafter the program generates the trust it needs to sustain itself.* We have rarely found insufficient trust to support experimentation with flexible working hours. Invariably, there are sections of an organization that are happy to participate in a pilot project. We have found that it then takes only six months to one year for all but the most suspicious supervisors to fully appreciate and accept the extent to which their subordinates in a well-designed plan can be trusted.

Trust is a necessary ingredient, a basic condition for OD activity. The induction of trust through flexible (and other rearranged) schedules is therefore a unique source of leverage that has not thus far been exploited. Flexible work hours can be used as an entry strategy in a comprehensive program of change in the direction of more extensive sharing of organizational responsibility and influence.

Flexible Schedules and Personal Competence

Comprehensive programs of change require individuals to acquire new skills as well as attitudes. When individuals are not competent to perform well in new situations, they feel inadequate and are therefore prone to resist change. Few people willingly expose themselves to the likelihood of failure. Mauk Mulder documented this phenomenon (1971) when he noted that worker members of boards of directors and works councils did not actually have much influence if they did not possess the skills necessary to function in those roles. Not only did workers take a back seat to more knowledgeable managers, but they felt worse about themselves as a result of participation in policy matters.

Skill training is a long and arduous process. Consequently, such changes as the redesign of jobs to enrich them often require major efforts at retraining. In contrast, flexible work schedules do not require the acquisition of new employee skills beforehand. An audit of work flows and work distribution should be done in preparation for an installation, as with all rearranged schedules, but prior extensive skill

---

* Other rearranged schedules may also lead to time periods where work is unsupervised. Under compressed-week systems, for example, supervisors may work standard hours while employees work an extended day. Under such a system, trust inducement is similar to the flexible hours system.

training is not necessary. The need for new skills emerges instead as experience with the new work schedules accumulates.

The need for new skills is often met by informal means, in the course of ordinary events as well as by special formal training programs. For example, in many installations, workers have trained each other in order to have coverage when they were absent. Commitment to cross-training was therefore higher and probably more meaningful than if it had been formally assigned. Supervisors have also been trained to do planning, at their request, when it has become clear that a shift in the nature of their work as the result of the new schedule required the acquisition of planning skills.

Felt Needs

Felt needs to which responses develop is a central ingredient of OD programs. Unless needs are addressed by a program, there is little likelihood that it will sustain itself. The model of identifying felt needs and responding to them is an old one, outlined in some detail by Elliott Jaques (1951) in his description and analysis of the Tavistock intervention at the Glacier Metal Company in England. In that instance, the consultants took some pains to get their resources advertised in the company and then waited for demands from particular sections of it for help in solving specific problems. As the consultants proved their worth, trust in them and their methods increased, leading eventually to a comprehensive program of change.

All of the methods in this book respond to felt needs of some employees—and where there has been high absenteeism or turnover, or low productivity, to the felt needs of managers for improving performance. The rigid nature of fixed schedules almost guarantees the existence of felt needs that the OD practitioner can effectively respond to with scheduling methods.

Furthermore, once installed, a flexible work schedules system generates needs to which the OD unit can respond. Since trust increases with the longevity of the arrangement, it becomes the foundation for other trust-based strategies of change.

After some time, supervisors learn that their subordinates can be trusted to schedule themselves to get the work done. Supervisory surveillance, then, and assignment of work by time, is decreased. Instead the supervisor must perform other functions. He or she must be prepared to give technical help, plan work flows and materials, coordinate with other departments, manage the distribution of information to facilitate subordinate decision-making and integration of differentiated tasks, and mediate when differences between individuals are not easily resolved. In addition, increased subordinate independence and more distant supervision requires more sophisticated criteria, standards, and measures of accomplishment.

As creatures of habit, accustomed to their own patterns of leadership, first-line supervisors rarely appreciate the need for prior training to meet anticipated demands arising from a shift to flexible schedules. Therefore, training in advance of need is unlikely to be effective. As the need for skills to cope with unexpected changes does emerge, an aware organization can make an informed response. It is also necessary, therefore, to set up a method of monitoring results that will provide the basis of designing appropriate interventions.

An impact on supervisory roles and functions is inevitable after a flextime installation. When subordinates sort themselves out to meet work loads, informally developing accommodating patterns of integration, pacing themselves, retraining each other, and making more on-line decisions about work, they assume responsibilities that were formerly probably solely within the province of their bosses. The shift in responsibility to lower levels also generates demand from them for more planning, technical help, and help in resolving interpersonal conflicts. In one instance we observed,

> . . . a supervisor in a bank who was essentially an accountant, struggled with problems with five clerks in his department who made telephone credit checks. Their workday previously started at 8:00 A.M. Before 8:00 the persons they contacted by telephone were not at work. When the clerks came in at 6:30 A.M., as permitted by the unit's new flexible hours plan, they had nothing to do, yet they preferred starting early to get out earlier than was previously possible. A review of the department's work distribution was needed in order to make productive work available to the clerks so that they could redistribute themselves according to their own and the department's needs. The clerks wanted to be productive, but they also wanted to take personal advantage of the flexible schedule arrangements. Except for the problem with starting time, the telephone work load distribution in a day did allow the clerks to vary their attendance. Though the supervisor was poorly equipped to audit his work flows and allocations, he

eventually managed to make meaningful work available before 8:00 A.M.

The supervisor was then confronted by interpersonal difficulties, which arose when the most senior clerk would not cooperate with her peers in shifting coverage to meet the variety of personal needs in the group as well as the demands of work. Faced with this conflict, the supervisor was again at sea. His accustomed response was bureaucratic. Left to his own devices, he would have set a schedule for everyone. Mediation was an unknown concept to him.

The supervisor's newly and acutely felt need for skills in planning and conflict management presented the bank with a golden opportunity to provide the kind of help that can blossom into a larger program of change.

The path of development in an OD program with an entry strategy of flexible schedules can follow the lines of pressure that flow upward from uncomfortable lower levels of an organization. A change in functions of subordinates forces changes in their supervisors. What was once done by them is absorbed by their workers. Supervisors must therefore seek new roles or resist the loss of old ones. Their search tends to erode the functions of those above them. A bottoms-up program of change that is comprehensive in scope can thus flow from what would appear to be a simple change in work schedules.

While an entry strategy from the bottom gradually forces the organization to respond, planned rather than random change requires top-level support. It is at this point that traditional notions about OD coincide with flexible schedules as an OD intervention. For us, OD does mean "planned change" whose scope is organization wide. We also agree with those theorists and practitioners who insist that significant and extensive change requires the support of those in the organization who are powerful. Without their protection and enthusiastic support, many an OD program has come to grief.

A SCENARIO FOR USE OF FLEXIBLE
WORKING HOURS AS AN ENTRY TO OD STRATEGY

As an aid to those who wish to plan OD efforts as a part of the introduction of altered work schedules, we have prepared a scenario that spells out how flexible hours might be incorporated as part of a larger OD plan. A similar scenario would be appropriate for the introduction of any, or a mix, of the scheduling methods.

1. Chief Executive Support

Assume top management is committed to a comprehensive program that will broaden the range of individual opportunities, increase access to resources, and produce reinforcing enabling structures. The objective is an increase in organizational effectiveness. It is a basic hypothesis of the planned change that increased commitment of employees to organizational goals is related to the perceived ability to influence them in ways that are personally meaningful. Therefore, there must be processes that increase individual control of tasks within accepted limits.

There is a wish to affect large numbers of the organization early in the program rather than at some time in a distant future.

2. Flexible Schedules—The Entry Point

After going through the DIPS analysis described in the previous chapter, a decision is made to use the concept of flexibility, in combination with as much choice of schedules as the system can tolerate, as an appropriate entry strategy. This will necessitate careful planning and involvement of many in the organization.

It is important to note that the methods chosen for selecting the scheduling innovation do not require an employee survey of preferences. Many organizations have learned to their regret that to ask for preferences is an intervention in itself, which often raises expectations of those queried. Unless the organization is genuinely prepared to act on the data it receives, it is probably better off not to ask at all.

Nevertheless, the organization need not choose schedules in the dark. Most, if not all, of the demographic, life-stage data discussed earlier in the book is available to organizations in its personnel files. Too few organizations have used such data to determine in advance the likely reactions of employees to innovations of all kinds. Contingency theories of management suggest that employee attitudes be taken into account in deciding upon appropriate management methods; insofar as attitudes are linked to demographics (including life stage), a great deal of inference and deduction can be done prior to raising the subject directly.

Of course, some organizations will be quite comfortable with whatever employees tell them, and will be happy to attempt to meet increased expectations, so that they will proceed with early surveying or interviewing. Since such openness is likely to foster further openness and trust, we certainly support it. But even in such responsive organizations, a bit of homework would not hurt, and might suggest new alternatives to ask about.

Once a scheduling method has been selected, managers at lower levels of the organization are then informed of the broad objectives of the program and the interest in beginning with the new work schedule.

Volunteers are solicited for a pilot project. The unit selected should be visible, have the support of direct supervisors, and have a sufficient number of tasks, the pace of which can be controlled by the individual, to permit a reasonable amount of flexibility. It is easier, of course, to be flexible in work units with low internal and external levels of interdependence. Since it is experience that the organization seeks to acquire, the first efforts should be with units that present sufficient challenge to be credible but not so much that success is problematical. Thus most routine white-collar work is well suited to flexible working hours, while a linear assembly line running on three shifts presents considerably more difficulty. Although assembly lines and continuous shift operations have been successfully adapted to flexible working hours, the preparation for them is fairly complex. Recourse to them should therefore come only after experience is accumulated in more simple areas. In general, for any change effort, success breeds success (Alinsky, 1972; Cohen and Gadon, 1978).

Once selected, the employees in a work unit should be informed, and interest in the proposed schedule surveyed. Before the schedule is introduced, there must be general acceptance of and support for it.

A technical audit of the work assignments and work flow should then be made by the immediate supervisor with internal or outside technical help, such as a production planner, capacity analyst, or procedures analyst. Arrangements should be made that will provide as many opportunities for the work force to be flexible as can be anticipated. Interaction with employees to be affected will increase their commitment as well as impart the very kinds of skills that will be needed by them and their supervisors.

A schedule should be set that fits the data compiled in the audit. Arrangements should be made for the length of the work day (band width), time recording, payment of overtime, treatment of holiday pay, and other schedule details as outlined in the chapter on flexible working hours.

A study group should be formed, composed of workers and managers from the full range of hierarchical levels in the organization, which will gather information on the pilot program on an ongoing basis. What is learned should be shared with top management and with the organization at large. As need emerges, interventions may be supported to meet them. These will probably include particular skills-training for supervisors, and internal information systems for the pilot work unit. Team-building activities might be appropriate as well as re-education of hourly workers. Especially at the end of the six-month trial, another audit should be conducted to compare roles, functions, and work flow with base line audit data.

A comparison of the structure of work before and after the schedule change will suggest the likely impact on supervisory behavior. In addition, there should be measures of performance against a variety of dimensions, including morale, productivity, quality, absenteeism (long and short-term), tardiness, turnover, accidents at work, and new ideas generated. The experiment should be evaluated and corrections made as indicated by results.

If results are favorable, plans can then be made to extend the schedule to other units, to include a significant percentage of the organization. Because large numbers would be covered, preparation for extension of the program will be more complex. Membership of the study group should be broadened. The inclusion of a high percentage of the hourly work force in the plan would generate needs for reconsideration of role and corresponding skills for the first level of supervision. Shifts in ways they functioned could then be met by planned efforts to reeducate the entire organization. At this point, the full range of OD technology is available, and a number of activities might be simultaneously used, including management training, team-building, job redesign, process consultation, and the like.

This scenario has many devices built into it designed to enhance trust, openness, shared influence, and choice regardless of whether the schedule experiment is successful. For example, the creation of a cross-section study group (with union representation where appropriate) allows for anticipation of difficulties, joint "ownership" of the innovation, open channels of information at all levels, and, if done properly, a willingness by management to make modifications based on feedback from employees as well as supervisors. The ex-

Months	*Possible Scenario*
0	Top managers meet and discuss alternative work schedules suggested by application of methods outlined in Chapter 6. Consider selection of work units in which experiment might be conducted. Criteria: limited interdependence, credibility, visibility, high probability of success. Conditions: no layoffs, limited experiment.
1	Meet with supervisors of eligible work units. Explain, solicit reactions, pick unit from volunteers.
1½	Meet with all employees in unit chosen for experiment. Explain, solicit reactions. If support from them, make commitment to proceed. Announce schedule for preparation for start date and keep employees informed of progress.
2	Set up *ongoing* study group composed of representatives from *all* levels of organization. Criteria for selection: Credibility, sympathy for values, understanding of concepts, skills to evaluate.
2	Roles of study group during trial: a) Data collection on: commitment, interpersonal relationships, satisfaction, productivity, absenteeism, tardiness, turnover, quality, work flows, cross-training, job coverage, job skill changes. b) Evaluation and recommendations to top management group. c) Dissemination of results.
2	*Start* training course for supervisors in experimental unit. Cover: anticipation of consequences, managerial functions, planning, conflict management, interdepartmental coordinating roles. Undertake technical audit in experimental unit.
3	Decide on range of flexibility allowed, rules, reporting, core time, payment of overtime, flextime, etc. Meet with all employees in experimental unit, inform them of schedule opportunities and constraints. Check for understanding and flaws in arrangements.
3	Start flexible work schedule in experimental unit.
3–9	Study group monitors results and feeds back information to improve results. Training provided as need arises to: first-level supervisors, hourly employees, second-level supervisors.

Months	Possible Scenario
	Information systems, service supplied as needed to support constructive changes.
10	Evaluation by study group: objectives, standards, measures, recommendations.
11	Evaluation by top management and decision to extend or abort.
11	Select units for extension of experiment—using persons in first experimental unit for support, information, education.
12	Start-up in additional work units selected—broaden membership of study group.

periences with such devices in projects supported by the Quality of Work Life Center suggest that they are likely to have important organizational payoffs regardless of what innovation is being introduced.

Many organizations have introduced flexible working hours and other rearranged workweek methods without such elaborate procedures. The methods are potent enough so that many benefits have been derived directly from them. But the unusual opportunities these methods offer for linking to and building further OD efforts have for the most part been lost as a result. It is ironic that those whose values are most compatible with the values intrinsic to the rearranged schedules, especially when employees may choose among them, have been so slow to see the possibilities in them. The introduction of any of the methods as a fad or gimmick may still improve individual lives and organizational functioning—a tribute to the potency of the methods—but further advantages are possible with careful planning and forethought.

CONCLUSION

OD efforts can be enhanced through the use of structural variables, such as *time*. Rearranged work schedules have value in and of themselves, but can also be introduced and utilized in ways that foster OD activities.

Choice among a variety of schedules can reinforce OD values. The utilization of flexible working hours, alone or in conjunction with other scheduling arrangements, is particularly useful for offering choices and inducing trust.

The utilization of rearranged schedules through methods involving vertical cross-sections of the organization presents new opportunities for OD practitioners to gain widespread credibility, move faster, and reach larger numbers of people in the organization.

Changing organizations is a difficult business; such opportunities should not be overlooked.

GLOSSARY

Adult Life Cycle

Stages of adult lives, beginning with the adolescent and post-adolescent years of sixteen to twenty-two. Studies suggest life stages of relative stability, lasting approximately seven years interrupted by periods of transition. Efforts have been made to associate predictable patterns of behavior with each period of stability and transition. Life stages have been characterized as:

Age	*Life Stage*
16–22	Breaking out
22/23–28	Establish self in the adult world
28–33	Time of transition—second thoughts about place in the adult world
30/33–40	Settling down
40–45	Mid-life crisis
45–55	Restabilization
55–65	Generativity (Emphasis on sharing rather than competition, teaching rather than striving, contemplation rather than doing)

Alternative Work Schedules

Work schedules other than the standard workweek of eight hours a day, five days a week, specifying the same starting and stopping time for each day for all employees in a given work unit.

Autonomous Work Group

A small group, consisting of usually between eight and twelve employees, in which employee relationships take place on a face-to-face basis, and where employees work on a relatively self-contained task (for example, a whole assembly such as for a watch (Omega) or a partial assembly such as an engine for an automobile (Saab)), and are responsible for a substantial range of scheduling, pacing, and work allocation decisions, without a formally designated management authority such as a foreman.

Band Width

The length of the work day in a flexible work hours schedule, starting with the earliest time that employees are allowed to report for work and ending with the latest time that a person may leave work. For instance, a person may work only eight hours in one day but may work within constraints established by the plan between a band width that has been set between 6:30 A.M. and 5:30 P.M.

Career Cycle

Stages through which adults pass in the course of their working lives. Studies suggest that predictable behavior patterns are associated with particular periods in the lives of working adults. Career stages have been characterized as:

Age	Career Stage
16–22	Exploration
22/23–28	Establishment
28–33	Granting of tenure
30/33–45	Maintenance, mid-career
45–55	Maintenance, late career
55–65	Decline
65 +	Retirement

Carryforward

A feature of some flexible hour work schedules, this arrangement allows a person to accumulate debit or credit balances of work time that can then be applied to a future reporting period. For instance, assume that the hours contracted to be worked are 37½ hours in a given workweek. The workweek is what is known as the reporting or accounting period. If debit and credit balances are allowed by the flexible work schedule, then a person might work only 35½ hours in one week and carry forward a debit balance of 2 hours. That person would owe the organization 2 hours, which could be made up by working 39½ hours in a future week.

Likewise, the person might carry forward a credit balance of 2 hours if he or she had worked 39½ hours in a given week. This would allow that person to work a 35½-hour week in the future without any loss in pay.

If carryforwards are allowed by a flexible work schedule, the plan usually stipulates the maximum debit or credit balances that can be carried forward. For 37½-hour contracted hours in a reporting period, the maximum debit and credit carryforward balances allowed are usually 2½ hours in order to avoid overtime payments required by wage and hour laws.

Compressed Week

Sometimes called 4 days/40 hours because of the prevalence of this particular configuration of a compressed-workweek schedule, the compressed week in fact covers a wider range of schedule arrangements.

The compressed week refers to any schedule that allows full-time work to be accomplished in fewer days than the standard five. By extending the length of the workday beyond the standard eight hours, a full week's worth of working time can be finished with 3 to 4½ days, allowing for more than the usual 2 days off. The extended "weekend," however, may come on any of the days of the week, depending on the particular compressed schedule followed. It is a method that usually yields many more three-day blocks of time off from work per year than do other rearranged workweek methods.

Core Time

Core time refers to those hours in the workday in a flexible hour schedule when everyone must be present. These hours reflect an analysis of work demands that indicate that a full complement of employees is required during particular times in a workday. Core time therefore represents the unique response to the particular work needs of an individual organization. In order to provide as complete opportunities as possible to take advantage of flexible hour scheduling, efforts are usually made to keep core times as short as possible.

Contracted Hours

Contracted hours refers to the number of hours a person agrees to work in a given period of time, known as the reporting or accounting period. It may be, for example, 40 hours in a week. Thus if the hours contracted to be worked were 40 hours in a week, a person might be allowed to vary the hours worked in any one day, within the constraints of the plan, so long as 40 hours were worked in the week. A workweek under such an arrangement might look as follows:

Days of week:	M	T	W	Th	F		Total
Hours worked:	6	10	8	10	6		40

Flexible Working Hours

Often called "flextime" or "flexitime," flexible working hours is essentially a work schedule that gives employees daily choice in the timing between work and nonwork activities. It is thus the only organizational arrangement that treats an individual as a whole person, with a life outside of work as well as in the organization. It is this characteristic of choice that distinguishes flexible working hours from all other work schedules. Because choice is its essence, it is not mutually exclusive, but can be combined with the other alternatives described in this book.

Flextime/Flexitime

Sometimes used interchangeably with the term flexible working hours to identify an entire scheduling plan, these terms also refer to those hours in a workday during which persons are allowed to decide for themselves whether to be present or absent. These are the periods of time within the band width that are outside of specified core times.

Floating Day

The floating day is a variation of a flexible working hour schedule distinguished by a reporting period confined to one day. Thus, with a floating day, a person must work all of his or her contracted hours in a given day. If the contract were for eight hours, then a person would have to work all of them each day. The choices an individual would have as to when they were worked would depend on the core and flexible time specifications for the workday.

Job Enlargement

An ambiguous phrase sometimes used interchangeably with job enrichment. Job enlargement usually refers to the increase in complexity of a job or the increase in cycle time needed for the completion of work through the combination of two or more jobs into one. It is distinguishable from job enrichment in the sense that work is not redesigned to take advantage of the motivational assumptions subsumed by job enrichment. Because job enlargement does not specifically build on the motivational assumptions of job enrichment, it does not have the motivating impact that job enrichment attempts to achieve.

Job Enrichment

Job enrichment refers to efforts to design work with the specific intention of building factors into it that have motivating power. The factors, which are assumptions about what is motivating about work, are autonomy, challenging work, variety, responsibility, advancement potential, and feedback.

Job Sharing

Job sharing is in a sense a variation of permanent part-time work, whereby two persons take responsibility for one job and divide the time they spend on it according to arrangements made with the employer. The arrangements may allow the two persons to decide how they will respectively allocate their time or they may specify the hours each person is to work.

Labor Force (Work Force)

These two phrases are used interchangeably. They refer to all persons who are willing and able to work and also actively seek employment. Ordinarily, these terms refer only to the civilian population, thus excluding persons who are in military service; the term "civilian labor force" specifically excludes persons in the military. The "labor force" or "work force" includes both all those employed, and all those who are unemployed. The term unemployed refers to all persons who are willing and able to work, who are actively seeking work, and who are unable to obtain gainful employment. It is not necessary for a person to apply for or to receive unemployment benefits to be included in the ranks of the unemployed.

Labor Force Participation Rate

The rate of participation in the labor force refers to the percentage of a given population who are willing and able to work and are actively seeking gainful employment. Thus the participation rate of women in the labor force in 1976 was 47.4 percent.

Organization Development

Organization development has been defined by Beckhard (1969) as "an effort (1) *planned* (2) *organization-wide*, and (3) *managed* from the top, to (4) increase *organization effectiveness* and *health* through (5) *planned interventions* in the organizations "processes," using *behavioral science* knowledge.

MBO (Management By Objectives)

MBO refers to systems of performance evaluation that involve persons in participation in goal setting for themselves, and in the identification of means to measure the achievement of those goals. The underlying assumptions of MBO are that persons will be more highly motivated to achieve goals if they are specific; if the persons affected have participated in the setting of the goals; if feedback is clear, relevant, and timely; and if the person evaluated has participated in determining the means of measurement of achievement of the goals.

Permanent Part-Time Work

From the organization's point of view, permanent part-time work refers to jobs that are available indefinitely on a part-time basis regardless of the tenure of the jobholder.

Though more enduring than casual part-time work, which lasts only for a season, it is often temporary from the point of view of individuals, serving a particular purpose, such as supplementing income while raising children, during a given time in their lives.

Reporting Period (Accounting Period)

Sometimes identified as the accounting period, the reporting period refers to the period during which contracted hours must be worked in a flexible work schedule. It may be one day, one week, one month, or even longer. In Europe a reporting period is not uncommon. In the

United States reporting periods are often confined to a day or a week because of the potential for overtime payments required by wage and hour laws.

Sabbatical

Sabbaticals refer to leaves of absence with pay. In academic circles they are commonly granted every seventh year for the purpose of providing faculty members with the opportunity to renew themselves. There is an apparent fit with the adult life cycle, associated with seven years of stability followed by a period of transition.

Scanlon Plans

Scanlon plans are gain-sharing plans that involve all employees in an organization in an effort to improve organizational effectiveness through the stimulation of suggestions and the evaluation of them by labor-management committees. Though often in organizations organized by labor unions, such plans are also in effect in nonunionized organizations.

Staggered Hours

Staggered hours are a variation of fixed, standard work weeks, which ordinarily consist of five consecutive eight-hour days in a given week with fixed start and stop times every day for all employees in a unit. In staggered hours, groups of employees are scheduled for different fixed start and stop times at given intervals, say, for instance, of fifteen minutes. Thus employees in department A might be scheduled to start at 7:00 A.M. and stop at 3:00 P.M., employees in department B scheduled to start at 7:15 A.M. and stop at 3:15 P.M., employees in department C scheduled to start at 7:30 A.M., and stop at 3:30 P.M., etc. The purpose of staggered hours is to even out demand on overloaded facilities, such as highways, public transportation, and parking.

Standard Workweek

The standard workweek refers to a workweek of five consecutive workdays of eight hours each, with fixed start and stop times for each day, for all employees in a given work unit.

Variable Hours

Variable hours is a variation of flexible work hours, usually referring to schedules in which there are no core times.

REFERENCES

Alinsky, Saul (1972). *Rules for Radicals.* New York: Vintage.

Argyris, Chris (1970). *Intervention Theory and Method.* Reading, Mass.: Addison-Wesley.

Bagchi, Pat (1976). "Job Sharing," *Peninsula Magazine* (Vol. 1, 6, April).

Beckhard, Richard (1969). *Organization Development: Strategies and Models.* Reading, Mass.: Addison-Wesley.

Bennett, Michael, Nicholas Dante, and James Kirkwood (1975). *A Chorus Line,* N.Y. Shakespeare Festival.

Best, Fred, and Barry Stern (1977). "Education, Work, and Leisure: Must They Come in That Order?" *Monthly Labor Review* 100, No. 7 (July): 3–9.

Blake, R. R., and J. S. Mouton (1964). *The Managerial Grid.* Houston: Gulf.

Bronson, Gail F. (1972). "Part-Time Professionals." *Wall Street Journal* (September 8).

Buisman, B. H. (1975). "The 4-day, 40-hour Workweek: Its Effect on Management and Labor." *Personnel Journal* 54 (November): 565–567.

Bureau of Labor Statistics (1977). "4-day, 40-hour Work-weeks" (March 17).

Catalyst Position Paper. "Construction of Employee Benefit Package for Part-Time Workers." Catalyst, Inc., N.Y.

Catalyst Position Paper. "Part-Time Social Workers in Public Welfare." Catalyst, Inc., N.Y. (October).

Cohen, Allan R., and Herman Gadon (1978). "Changing the Management Culture in a Public School System." *Journal of Applied Behavioral Science* 14, No. 1: 61–78.

Committee on Alternative Work Patterns and National Center for Productivity and Quality of Working Life (1976). *Alternatives in the World of Work*. Washington, D.C.: U.S. Government Supt. of Documents (Winter).

Comptroller General of U.S.A. (1976). "Part-Time Employment in Federal Agencies." *Changing Patterns of Work in America*. Washington, D.C.: U.S. Government Printing Office. (See Owen (1976) for full reference)

Cross, Wilbur (1971). "The Four-Day Work Week is Coming Sooner Than You Think." *Business Management* 40 (April): 14–15.

Cummings, Thomas G., and Edmond S. Molloy (1977). *Improving Productivity and the Quality of Work Life*. New York: Praeger.

Cunningham, Alice (1976). Testimony to U.S. Senate Subcommittee on Employment, Poverty and Migratory Labor, of the Committee on Labor and Public Welfare, Washington, D.C. Published as *Changing Patterns of Work in America,* Washington, D.C., U.S. Government Printing Office.

Darrow, Susan T., and S. L. Stokes (1973). "Part Time Professional Employment in Three Settings at the University of Michigan." University of Michigan Center for Continuing Education of Women (August).

Davis, Sheldon, and Richard Walton. "Maximizing Improvement in the Quality of Work Life and Organizational Productivity." Speech at OD Network Conference, May 1977, Portsmouth, New Hampshire.

deChalendar, Jacques. *L'Aménagement du Temps: Flextime*. Thesis, DesClée De Brouwer.

Dobelis, M. C. (1972). "The 3-day Week—Offshoot of an E.D.P. Operation." *Personnel* 49 (January–February): 24–33.

Dunham, R. B., and D. L. Hawk (1977). The Four-Day/Forty-Hour Week: Who Wants It? *Academy of Management Journal* 20, No. 4.

Elbing, Alvar O., Herman Gadon, and John Gordon (1974). "Flexible Working Hours: It's About Time." *Harvard Business Review* 52 (January–February): 18–33.

Employment and Training Report of the President, 1976. Superintendent of Documents, U.S. Government Printing Office, Washington, D.C.

Erickson, E. H. (1959). "Identity and the Life-Cycle." *Psychological Issues* 1: 1–171.

Etzioni, Amitai (1977). "Opting Out: The Waning of the Work Ethic." *Psychology Today* 11 (July): 18.

Evans, Christopher (1976). "A Way to Improve Office's Efficiency: Just Stay at Home." *Wall Street Journal* (December 14).

Eyde, Lorraine (1975). "Flexibility Through Part Time Employment of Career Women in the Public Service." U.S. Civil Service Commission Professional Series, 75-3 (June).

Fottler, Myron (1977). "Employee Acceptance of a Four-Day Workweek." *Academy of Management Journal* 20, No. 4.

Feron, James (1974). "A Chrysler Union Drops 4-Day Week." *New York Times* (October 6).

Freedman, Marcia (1976). *Labor Markets: Segments and Shelters.* New York: Osman.

Galbraith, Jay R. (1977). *Organization Design.* Reading, Mass.: Addison-Wesley, Chapter 15.

Gallese, Liz Roman (1977). "The Green Dream: Vermont Life Proves Austere but Satisfying for Former Urbanites." *Wall Street Journal* (August 18).

Glueck, William F. (1977). "Changing Hours of Work: A Review and Analysis of the Research." Paper delivered at the Academy of Management, Orlando, Florida (August 15).

Golembiewski, Robert T., Rick Hilles, and Munro S. Kagno (1974). "A Longitudinal Study of Flexi-Time Effects: Some Consequences of an O.D. Structural Intervention." *Journal of Applied Behavioral Science* 10, No. 4 (October–December): 503–532.

Gould, Roger (1975). "Adult Life Stages." *Psychology Today* 18 (February): 74–78.

Greenwald, Carol (1973). "Part-Time Workers Can Bring Higher Productivity." *Harvard Business Review* 51 (September): 20.

Hackman, J. R., and G. R. Oldham (1974). *The Job Diagnostic Survey.* Technical Report No. 4., Department of Administrative Sciences, Yale University.

Hackman, J. Richard, and J. L. Suttle (1977). *Improving Life at Work.* Santa Monica: Goodyear.

Haller, Willi (1977). "Flexyear: The Ultimate Work Hour Concept." Reproduced by Interflex, Inc., New York City.

Harbridge House (1977). "Evaluation of Pilot Flexible Working Hours Program. Commonwealth of Massachusetts, 1976" (February 15).

Hayghe, Howard V., and Kopp Michelotti (1971). "Multiple Job-Holding in 1970–71." *Monthly Labor Review* 94 (October): 38–45.

Hedges, Janice (1971). "A Look at the Four-day Workweek." *Monthly Labor Review* 94 (October): 33–37.

Hedges, Janice (1973). "New Patterns for Working Time." *Monthly Labor Review* 96 (February): 3–8.

Hedges, Janice (1975). "How Many Days Make a Workweek?" *Monthly Labor Review* 98 (April): 29–36.

Herzberg, Frederick (1966). *Work and the Nature of Man.* Cleveland, Ohio: World.

Hoffman, Eileen (1972). "The Four-Day Week Raises New Problems." *The Conference Board Record* (February).

Hoffman, L. W., and F. I. Nye (1974). *Working Mothers: An Evaluation Review of the Consequences for Wife, Husband and Child.* San Francisco: Jossey-Bass.

Homans, George C. (1961). *Social Behavior; Its Elementary Forms.* New York: Harcourt.

International Labor Organization, Geneva (1973). "Part-Time Employment: An International Survey" (December).

Ivancevich, J., and H. Lyon. "The Shortened Workweek: A Field Experiment." *Journal of Applied Psychology* (forthcoming).

Jackson, John H., T. J. Keaveny, and R. E. Allen (1977). "An Examination of Preferred Job Characteristic Differences in Part-Time and Full-Time Workers." Paper delivered at Academy of Management, Kissimee, Florida (August).

Jaques, Elliot (1951). *The Changing Culture of the Factory.* New York: Dryden.

Kanter, Rosabeth Moss (1977a). *Men and Women of the Corporation.* New York: Basic Books.

Kanter, Rosabeth Moss (1977b). "Work in a New America." *Daedalus* 106 (Fall).

Kriedt, Philip H. (1973). "The Rearranged Workweek: Prudential's Experience." *Personnel Quarterly* (August).

Kronholtz, June (1977). "Baby Boomlet?" *Wall Street Journal* (July 29).

Levine, James A. (1977). "Part-Time Work." *Working Woman* (March).

Levinson, Daniel J. (1977). "The Mid-life Transition: A Period in Adult Psychosocial Development." *Psychiatry* 40, No. 2 (May): 99–112.

Levitan, Sar S., and Richard S. Belous (1977). "Reduced Work Time: An Alternative to High Unemployment." George Washington University, Washington, D.C.

"Job Sharing in Libraries: Report from Massachusetts" (1976). *Library Journal* (November 15).

Lublin, Joann S. (1977a). "Blues in the Night: 'Graveyard' Shift Cuts Kohler Co. Power Bills, But Irks Some Workers." *Wall Street Journal* (October 18).

Lublin, Joann (1977b). "Shifting the Load; New Electricity Rates Could Have Big Effect on Prices and People." *Wall Street Journal* (August 12).

Mahoney, T. A., J. Newman, and P. Frost (1975). "Workers' Perceptions of the Four-day Week." *California Management Review* 18, No. 1 (Fall): 21–35.

Main, Jeremy (1977). "Good Jobs Go Part Time." *Money* 6 (October): 80–82.

Maklan, David Mark (1977). "How Blue-Collar Workers on 4-day Workweeks Use Their Time." *Monthly Labor Review* 100, No. 8 (August): 18–26.

Mangum, Garth L. (1976). *Employability, Employment and Income.* Salt Lake City: Olympus.

Manpower Report of the President, 1975. Washington, D.C.: Superintendent of Documents, U.S. Government Printing Office.

Martin, Virginia H. (1974). "Recruiting Women Managers Through Flexible Hours." *S.A.M. Journal* 39, No. 3 (July): 46.

McGregor, Douglas (1960). *The Human Side of Enterprise.* New York: McGraw-Hill.

Meredith, Jane L. (1966). *Part Time Employment for Women.* Washington, D.C.: U.S. Department of Labor, Woman's Bureau, 1966.

Michelotti, Kopp (1975). "Multiple Jobholders in May, 1975." *Monthly Labor Review* 98 (November): 56–62.

Mintzberg, Henry (1975). "The Manager's Job: Folklore and Fact." *Harvard Business Review* 53, No. 4 (July–August): 49–61.

Morgan, F. T. (1977). "Your (Flex)Time May Come." *Personnel Journal* 56, No. 2 (February): 82.

Mulcahy, Sheila Hogan (1976). "Testimony to Wisconsin State Legislature Committee on Part-Time and Flexible-Time Employment" (September 23).

Mulder, Mauk (1971). "Power Equalization Through Participation?" *Administration Science Quarterly* 16, No. 1.

Nathan, Robert Stuart (1977). "The Scheme That's Killing the Rat-Race Blues." *New York* (July 18).

"Women At Work" (1976). *Newsweek* (December 6).

"The Graying of America" (1977). *Newsweek* (February 28).

"Job Sharing in Schools." *New Ways to Work*, rev. ed. 1976.

"The Four-Day Work Week: A Much Praised Idea That Few Want to Try" (1977). *New York Times* (August 28).

Nollen, Stanley, B. Eddy, V. H. Martin, and D. Monroe (1976). "Permanent Part-Time Employment; An Interpretive Review." Georgetown University (February).

Nord, W. R., and R. Costigan (1973). "Worker Adjustment to the 4-day Week: A Longitudinal Study." *Journal of Applied Psychology* 58: 60–66.

Oakes, Imogene E. (1972). *Adult Education Participants and Participation.* National Center for Educational Statistics.

Olmstead, B. (1977). "Job Sharing—A New Way to Work." *Personnel Journal* 56, No. 2 (February): 78–81.

Owen, J. D. (1976). "The Long Run Prospects for Alternative Work Schedules." *Changing Patterns of Work in America.* Hearings before the Subcommittee on Employment, Poverty and Migratory Labor of the Committee on Labor and Public Welfare, United States Senate (April 7 and 8).

Pigors, Paul, and Faith Pigors (1944). *Human Aspects of Multiple Shift Operations.* Cambridge, Mass.: M.I.T. Press.

Poor, Riva (Ed.) (1973). *4 days, 40 hours and Other Forms of the Rearranged Work Week.* New York: Mentor.

Poor, Riva, and James L. Steele (1973). "Work and Leisure: The Reactions of People at 4-Day Firms." *4 days, 40 hours.* New York: Mentor.

Pryblek, Wilma (1974). "Are the CPI Ready for Three-day Workweek?" *Chemical Engineer* (April 1).

Quinn, R. P., and H. Sheppard (1971). *Survey of Working Conditions.* University of Michigan Survey Research Center for the U.S. Department of Labor.

Raskin, A. H. (1975). "Whatever Happened to the 4-Day Week." *New York Times* (January 19).

Raskin, A. H. (1976). "Breakthrough on Work Hours." *New York Times* (October 8).

Riddell, Stead and Associates (1973). "Report on the Altered Work Week" (November).

Roberts, B. (1975). *Middle-Aged Career Dropouts: An Exploration.* Unpublished doctoral dissertation, Brandeis University.

Robison, David (1977). "Control Data's Selby Bindery Plant Employs 100% Part-Time Staff of Mothers and Students." *World of Work Report* 2, No. 9 (September).

Roper Reports (1974). "Work: Desires, Discontents and Satisfactions." Special Report (June).

Schein, E. H. (1971). "The Individual, the Organization, and the Career: A Conceptual Scheme." *Journal of Applied Behavioral Science* 7: 401–426.

Schein, E. H. (1975). "How Career Anchors Hold Executives to their Career Paths." *Personnel* 52: 11–24.

Schein, E. H. (1978). *Career Dynamics: Matching Individual and Organizational Needs.* Reading, Mass.: Addison-Wesley.

Schein, Virginia (1976). "Metropolitan Life Insurance Company." In David Robison (Ed.), *Alternative Work Patterns,* Work In America Institute.

Schonberger, Richard J. (1970). "Ten Million U.S. Housewives Want to Work." *Labor Law Journal* 21 (June 21): 374–379.

Sease, Douglas R. (1977). "Construction Unions in Jacksonville, Fla., Strike Novel Accord." *Wall Street Journal* (August 30).

Sheehy, Gail (1974). *Passages.* New York: Dutton.

Sheppard, Harold L. (1976). "Government's Role in Improving the Quality of Work-Life." *Changing Patterns of Work in America.* Hearings before the Subcommittee on Employment, Poverty and Migratory Labor of the Committee on Labor and Public Welfare, U.S. Senate, Washington, D.C.

Silverberg, Marjorie M. (1972). "Part Time Careers in the Federal Government." *The Bureaucrat* (Fall).

Sprague, Linda G. (1973). "Fewer Days or Fewer Hours." In Riva Poor (Ed.), *4 days, 40 hours.* New York: Mentor.

Steers, Richard J. (1977). "Antecedents and Outcomes of Organizational Commitment." *Administration Science Quarterly* 22 (March): 46–56.

Stein, Barry A., Allan R. Cohen, and Herman Gadon (1976). "Flextime: Work When You Want To." *Psychology Today* 10 (June): 40–41.

Strauss, George (1974). "Workers, Attitudes and Adjustments." In Jerome M. Rosow (Ed.), *The Worker and His Job.* Englewood Cliffs, N.J.: Prentice-Hall.

Sum, Andrew M. (1977). "Female Labor Force Participation: Why Projections Have Been Too Low." *Monthly Labor Review* 100 (July): 17–24.

Super, D. E. (1957). *The Psychology of Careers.* New York: Harper & Row.

Swerdloff, Sol (1975). "The Revised Workweek: Results of a Pilot Study of 16 Firms." U.S. Department of Labor, Bureau of Labor Statistics, Bulletin 1846.

Temporary State Commission on Management and Productivity in the Public Sector (1976). *An Introduction to Alternative Work Schedules.* Albany, N.Y. (August).

"The Quality of Work Program: The First Eighteen Months" (1975). National Quality of Work Center and the Institute for Social Research, Ann Arbor, Michigan.

"Two for the Price of One; Job-Sharing" (1976). *Time* (May 3).

U.S. Civil Service Commission (1974). *Women in Action*. Washington, D.C.

U.S. Department of Commerce (1973). *Statistical Abstract of the U.S.*

Van Maanen, John, and Edgar Schein (1977). "Career Development." In Hackman and Suttle (Eds.), *Improving Life at Work*. Santa Monica, Ca.: Goodyear.

"Remote Terminals Let Handicapped Workers Program Computers at Home" (1977). *Wall Street Journal* (August 30).

"Weekend Jobs Work Out Just Fine for Part-time Workers" (1977). *Wall Street Journal* (August 23).

Weinstein, Harriet Goldberg (1975). *A Comparison of Three Alternative Work Schedules: Flexible Work Hours, Compact Work Week, and Staggered Work Hours*. Thesis. Industrial Research Unit, Wharton School, University of Pennsylvania.

Wirtz, Willard (1975). *The Boundless Resource*. Washington, D.C.: New Republic.

Work in America (1973). Cambridge, Mass.: The MIT Press.

"Teenage Unemployment Remains High; Carter Proposes Labor Market Plan" (1977). *World of Work Report* 2, No. 6.

Yankelovich, Daniel (1974a). *The New Morality; A Profile of American Youth in the 1970's*. New York: McGraw-Hill.

Yankelovich, Daniel (1974b). "The Meaning of Work." In Jerome M. Rosow (Ed.), *The Worker and the Job: Coping with Change*. Englewood Cliffs, N.J.: Prentice-Hall.

Young, Anne McDougall (1977a). "Students, Graduates and Dropouts in the Labor Market, 1976." *Monthly Labor Review* 100, No. 7 (July): 40–43.

Young, Anne McDougall (1977b). "Going Back to School at 35 and Over." *Monthly Labor Review* 100, No. 7 (July): 43–45.